THE ART OF NOT SELLING

Gerald Gordon Clerx

Copyright © 2016 G. Gordon Clerx
All rights reserved.

PREFACE

Our global economy is in transition and so too is the sales profession. *Competition* has given way to *collaboration*; *closing* has given way to *opening*; *selling* has given way to *partnering*.

To successfully navigate this new consumer landscape your **attitude** must be rooted in a partnership mentality, your **aptitude** must include a complete understanding of your client's needs and your **actions** must align with your client's goals and decision-making criteria.

This book will introduce you to the Gap Analysis Client Engagement Model©. This model is not just a strategy for partnering success; it is a strategy for relationship and leadership success as well.

At its essence it's about providing others with a safe passage through challenging circumstances. The better we all understand it … the more we all embrace it and consistently deliver it ... the greater the effect we make in this world and the more we all get in return.

As a colleague of mine Zig Ziglar once said, *"To get whatever you want in life, simply help enough other people get what they want in life."*

The content of this book will help you get more of what **you** want in **your** life by giving you the insights, skills and resources to help your clients get more of what **they** want in **their** lives.

Is This Book For Me?

If you are in a client/ customer facing role, then **YES!** …**Unequivocally, unashamedly, unreservedly YES!**

Excuse my apparent lack of humility but the reason why I say that with such certainty and conviction is because that is what thousands of course graduates have said about the content within this book and how it has accelerated their careers. When you have something that you know will enhance the lives of others, it's appropriate to be **BOLD**.

This book has been created for one purpose; *to accelerate YOUR professional success*, regardless of how many years you've been in the business. If you are new to the sales profession then this book represents a fresh clearing from which to launch a successful career. Those new to the business often get the best traction from core competency skill training because they have no "old school" habits to unlearn.

If you are more experienced your professional role, you too will benefit tremendously from the contents found within. For you, this book represents a transition point in your career because regardless of how successful you have been to date, you will experience far greater success from this point forward.

Yes, it's true that you might have to unlearn some OLD school techniques that are no longer relevant in this NEW market economy but they will be replaced by a fresh set of practical skills and insights that are immediately applicable. The most common comment I receive from my more senior course graduates of this training series is, "This is the finest training I have received in my 20+ years in the business."

In fact, I believe so strongly in the content of this book that I will back my words with an unconditional guarantee. If you don't think the strategies in this book will immediately accelerate your professional success then return it for a full, no questions asked, refund.

So "*Yes*" ... this book is definitely for you! That's why it has found its way into your hand or onto your screen! Read it and take immediate control of your professional career.

Gerald Gordon Clerx

DEDICATION

This book is dedicated to my inspiring wife and
business partner Shell, who is unrelenting
in her support toward my work.
Also to my three amazing children
Brayden, Sterling, and Alexia,
who remind me every day to
think BIG, be BOLD, and
DANCE like no one's watching.

INTRODUCTION

The GAP

The global economic downturn marked a critical crossroad for those within the sales profession. This event forever altered the consumer landscape and the client engagement model required to successfully navigate it.

Today, consumers are more skeptical, price conscious, product savvy and pressure resistant than at any other time in history. They don't want to be *cold called*, *up sold*, or *hard sold*. They don't want to be *trial closed*, *tie down closed*, or *Columbo closed*. They don't want *loss leaders*, *red herrings*, or *high pressure*. And they certainly don't want to be *nibbled*. These "old school" sales tactics have no place in this new consumer landscape.

A fresh new "partnership" approach to engaging clients has officially trumped the old "salesmanship" approach of years past, and those organizations that make this transition will thrive and survive in this new global economy. Those who fail to adapt will continue to lose clients and soon find themselves out of business!

The BRIDGE

A bridge serves a truly noble purpose: it takes people from *where they are* to *where they want to get to*, directly, reliably and consistently. Each one spans a gap, often over perilous terrain, offering its users a quicker and safer alternative to get to their desired destination.

This book serves a similar purpose: to take you from where you are in your career, to where you want to be, without having to endure the lost time and forfeited revenues resulting from failed client experiences. As Groucho Marx once said; "We should learn from the mistakes of others. We don't have time to make them all ourselves."

– This book is YOUR success bridge! –

Although I am the architect of the Gap Analysis Client Engagement Model©, I give much of the credit to the thousands of success partners and service providers whom I've met and trained over the years. Throughout the learning process, each one of them has helped to shape the model into its current form.

The stories I tell are real; the results I promise are achievable and in fact have been achieved by success partners from around the globe. This training series has been delivered in twenty-eight countries to over eighty thousand success partners, many who now generate commissioned earnings in excess of two million dollars annually.

The one common thread linking top producers in any market is that they do three things better than their competitors. These three skill sets represent the core competencies of client engagement: ASSESSMENT, PRESENTATION and NEGOTIATION.

As a point of fact, your professional success is a direct reflection of your competence in *assessing* client needs, *presenting* compelling solutions, and *negotiating* collaborative outcomes. After all, this represents the value you bring to your profession and the more competent you are, the more sales success you'll experience. It's as simple as that!

'The Fine Art of NOT Selling' is three books in one.

In **Part I** you'll master the first core skill of engagement: ASSESSMENT. In this part of the book, you will discover exactly what questions to ask to fully uncover the gap between your client's *current reality* condition and *desired reality* outcome. You'll also learn how to identify your client's engagement style so that you'll understand what he or she needs to experience in your offering to support a favorable buying decision.

In **Part II** you'll master the second core skill of engagement: PRESENTATION. Your ability to align your product or service message with your client's unique decision-making needs sits at the core of a successful transaction. In this part of the book you'll learn how to tailor your *content, structure* your message and strengthen your *delivery*.

In **Part III** you'll master the third core skill of client engagement: NEGOTIATION. In this part of the book, you will discover the three potential deal breakers of every negotiation, how to recognize them, and more importantly, how to respond to them when they are encountered.

The Gap Analysis Client Engagement Model© is helping success partners 'bridge their success gap' at a global level. Those who have applied the skills and insights from this book have experienced an immediate and dramatic increase in their business win rate and customer satisfaction levels.

Now for the first time, the principles of the Gap Analysis Client Engagement Model© is available to you in this landmark book and timely book. **Read it and seize immediate control of your professional career!**

CONTENTS

Preface   *iii*
Is this book for me?   *v*
Dedication   *vii*
Introduction   *ix*

PART I ~ THE ASSESSMENT PHASE

Introduction to ASSESSMENT   2

Chapter One – Introduction to Engagement Styles   5
Accelerate your professional success by aligning your business activities with your preferred style of engagement.
    What Is My Engagement Style   6
    I'm Definitely a 'Director'   10
    I'm Totally a 'Connector'   15
    I Feel I'm a 'Supporter'   20
    I Think I'm an 'Analyzer'   25

Chapter Two - Assessing Your Client's Engagement Style   30
Accelerate your professional success by recognizing your client's preferred style of engagement.
    Tuning in to Your Client   31
    How to Recognize 'Directors'   35
    How to Recognize 'Connectors'   40
    How to Recognize 'Supporters'   46
    How to Recognize 'Analyzers'   51

Chapter Three - Assessing Your Client's Gap   56
Accelerate your professional success by isolating your client's product or service gap.
    Seek First to Understand   57
    Where Are You Going   61

Where Are You Now   66

PART II ~ THE PRESENTATION PHASE

Introduction to PRESENTATION   73

Chapter Four – Crafting Your Message   77
Accelerate your professional success by convincing logically and inspiring emotionally.
    Ladies and Gentleman of the Jury   78

Chapter Five - Aligning Your Content   86
Accelerate your professional success by aligning your offering with your client's decision-making needs.
    Engaging a 'Director' Client   87
    Engaging a 'Connector' Client   92
    Engaging a 'Supporter' Client   96
    Engaging an 'Analyzer' Client   100
    Differentiate Yourself   104

Chapter Six - Strengthening Your Delivery   107
Accelerate your professional success with presentations that are memorable and impact-full.
    You've Got Thirty Seconds … GO   108

PART III ~ THE NEGOTIATION PHASE

Introduction to NEGOTIATION   117

Chapter Seven – Recognizing Negotiating Stress   120
Accelerate your professional success by recognizing the three sources of a failed negotiation.
    Three TITANIC Deal Breakers   121
    Recognizing *Mental* Stress   128
    Recognizing *Emotional* Stress   132

Recognizing *Positional* Stress   136

Chapter Eight - Resolving Negotiating Stress   139
Accelerate your professional success by resolving the three conditions of negotiating stress.
    The ACRE Formula©   140
    ACRE Eliminates *Mental* Stress   144
    ACRE Diffuses *Emotional* Stress   151
    ACRE Resolves *Positional* Stress   157

After the Deal is Done   165
Accelerate your on-going professional success by relentlessly fine-tuning your product/ service offering.
    How Did I Do   166

Summary   171
Speaking Engagements   172

PART 1

THE ASSESSMENT PHASE

In this first part of the book you will learn how to *align* your business, *identify* your clients and comprehensively *assess* their product/ service gap.

Introduction to Assessment

The first phase of the Gap Analysis Client Engagement Model© is the ASSESSMENT Phase.

- Have you ever had a client fail to take action on a product or service offering that she should have acquired?
- Have you ever spent a lot of time with a client who you later discovered had neither the finances nor motivation to take action?
- Have you ever had a client tell you exactly what he wanted and yet went out and bought something completely different ... from one of your competitors?

... If you answered 'yes' to any of these questions then you've suffered the consequences of a failed client assessment. Know with absolute certainty that the success of your product or service offering is built upon the foundation of your initial client assessment.

ASSESSMENT TIP:

The success of your product/ service proposal is built upon the foundation of your initial client assessment.

A well-conducted assessment provides you with a solid footing from which to design and deliver a custom tailored and product-specific presentation. Reflect on that fact, because it's critical to your success that you understand it. You can't confidently prescribe a solution if you haven't accurately diagnosed the problem.

The purpose of this part of the book is to accelerate your success by providing you with the **insights**, **skills**, and **resources** *to align your business, assess your clients and clarify their requirements.*

In Chapter One you'll be introduced to an assessment tool that will help to establish your preferred style of engagement. Armed with this information you'll be better able to define your personal brand and align your professional activities accordingly to ensure a successful and enduring career.

You will discover that your unique engagement style has specific *strengths* and *limitations* which, when understood, enables you to structure your business activities and professional partnerships accordingly.

In Chapter Two you'll learn how to uncover your client's preferred style of engagement by observing *verbal, vocal,* and *visual* communication patterns.

You've no doubt discovered that people are different. You can say one thing to one client and he will feel utterly compelled to take action, yet that identical message delivered to another will leave her completely uninspired. Why is that? It all comes down to differences in engagement styles. A client's style influences what needs to be *heard, seen* and *known* to justify a purchase decision.

In Chapter Three you'll learn a questioning strategy designed to accurately define your client's *current reality* situation and *desired reality* outcome.

As a success partner you must have absolute certainty on both these reference points. Why? Because the difference between them represents the gap! This gap constitutes the problem, which can only be successfully bridged if both coordinates are known.

Depending on the complexity of your product or service offering it might be necessary to obtain over fifty combined pieces of information to fully assess your client's gap. Anything less would constitute an inconclusive assessment and compromise your ability to present a valid and compelling solution.

The Acceleration Strategies that follow will provide you with the tools, insights and resources to master the core skill of ASSESSMENT.

THE ASSESSMENT PHASE

~Chapter One~

Introduction To Engagement Styles

Accelerate a successful client experience by aligning your business activities with your preferred style of engagement.

༄

"What you are speaks so loudly, I can't hear what you are saying."
—Ralph Waldo Emerson

> "Engagement styles helps us to understand why we do what we do ... and why others don't."
> – G. Gordon Clerx

WHAT IS MY ENGAGEMENT STYLE

The way you engage with others influences how they, in turn, interact with you. You'll know this to be true. Think about it: you naturally hit it off with some clients—you establish instant rapport—you speak in a way that is easy for them to hear and in a way that they need to hear it. In fact, everything you do, think, and say is in alignment with the client and the engagement experience unfolds effortlessly.

Unfortunately the opposite is also true. You can likely recall times interacting with a client with whom you were completely out of sync. In this instance, nothing seemed to flow and the experience was mentally and emotionally draining.

So how do you determine your engagement style? Our on-line test would take about ten minutes to complete. However, you can also get considerable insight into your style by reflecting on the following sets of descriptive adjectives and selecting the group that you feel best describes you, in your current professional role.

- The *first* group of descriptive adjectives is 'demanding, ambitious, daring, restless, and assertive'.
- The *second* group of descriptive adjectives is 'influencing, optimistic, enthusiastic, persuading, and charming'.

- The *third* group is 'steady, deliberate, patient, accommodating, and sincere'.
- The *fourth* group is 'cautious, logical, precise, doubting, and perfectionist'.

If you feel the first group best describes you then write down or remember the word 'Director'. This is your primary style descriptor. If you feel the second group best describes you overall then write down or remember the word 'Connector'. If it is the third group then write down the word 'Supporter' and if the forth group, the word 'Analyzer'.

Now reflect again on the remaining three sets of descriptive adjectives. Select the group that is second most like you. This is your secondary style descriptor. Once you know your *primary* and *secondary* behavioral characteristics you will begin to see why you connect with some people and why you don't with others.

Director

If you selected the first group of descriptors as being most like you then your primary style group is 'Director'.

Directors are *actively* paced and *outcome* focused. They are often found in leadership positions; because that is their preferred role.

Connector

If you selected the second list of descriptors and as being most like you then your primary style group is 'Connector'.

Connectors are *actively* paced and *socially* focused. They are often found in the sales profession, in public relation positions, or in the role of talk show hosts.

Supporter

If you selected the third group of descriptors as being

most like you then your primary style group is 'Supporter'.

Supporters are *passively* paced (deliberate) and *socially* focused. They are typically found in occupations or roles that are in service to others. The health care industry and teaching professions are both strongly represented by members of this style group.

Analyzer

If you selected the fourth list of descriptors as being most like you then your primary style group is 'Analyzer'.

Analyzers are *passively* paced (methodical) and *task* focused. Since Analyzers are strongly policy and procedure driven, we typically find them in highly structured professions or roles. The accounting and engineering professions are dominated by members of this style group, as too are those in CFO positions.

In the following four Acceleration Strategies, I will introduce you to the naturally occurring strengths and limitations of each engagement style so that you can recognize them within yourself and structure your business accordingly.

ASSESSMENT ACTION PLAN

○━ INSIGHTS:

Know that your engagement style impacts how you sell, how clients respond to you and the strengths you bring to your profession.

○━ SKILLS:

Apply engagement style awareness to help you structure your business to align with your natural occurring engagement strengths.

> *"If winning isn't everything, why do they keep score?"*
> – Vince Lombardi

I'M DEFINITELY A 'DIRECTOR'

Do you dislike losing, refuse to wait in line, loathe being told what to do, and resent having someone else be in control of your physical environment? These are some of the characteristics that define this style group.

Directors prefer a fast-paced environment that is ripe with challenges. Let's look at some of the behavioral assets and liabilities of Directors.

Behavioral assets of Directors include the ability to:

- ☺ Generate results in the face of opposition
- ☺ Figure out ways to move the process forward
- ☺ Question the status quo and implementing new standards accordingly
- ☺ Take on challenging situations with confidence and speed
- ☺ Lead others toward a common goal

Directors accelerate their success by their naturally occurring abilities during each of the three phases of the Gap Analysis Client Engagement Model©:

> During the ASSESSMENT phase, Directors are highly skilled at getting right to the point. They don't waste time and aren't afraid to ask pointed and probing questions to accurately and efficiently uncover the client's requirement.

During the PRESENTATION phase, Directors are known to communicate the merits of their offering in a bold and forthright manner. They speak with certainty and conviction, instilling confidence in others. They are also very efficient in their use of time and are not afraid to ask for the business at the conclusion of their presentation.

During the NEGOTIATION phase, Directors are skilled at overcoming opposition. They are outcome-oriented and constantly move the ball toward the goal line. If they encounter resistance during their end zone drive they're not afraid to push through the obstacle, however challenging. A common Director response to a stalled negotiation is "Leave it with me and I'll figure something out" or "What's it going to take to get the deal done?"

Directors are especially effective when engaged in activities that align with their naturally direct approach.

ASSESSMENT TIP:

Directors are especially effective when engaged in activities that align with their naturally direct approach.

Just as Directors have naturally occurring behavioral assets, so too do they have behavioral liabilities that can hinder their professional success. These include a tendency to:

- ☹ Be impatient with the behavior of other styles
- ☹ Communicate in a blunt and often sarcastic manner
- ☹ Find fault in others' actions or inactions
- ☹ Resist participation in a team, unless in a leadership role
- ☹ Override the opinions and actions of others

There are three Director style group pairings. They include:

The 'Connecting Director'

If your style pairing is primary Director with secondary Connector, then you are known to combine the qualities of *friendliness* and *persuasion* with *competitiveness* and *directness*. Richard Branson, Ronald Reagan, and Mark Cuban are thought to share this pairing. If this is your style group then your greatest asset is your ability to come up with unique and imaginative solutions to gaps in the market.

As a member of this style group, you have been gifted with the ability to gain the willing cooperation of others, which makes you extremely effective at encouraging others to follow your lead. In a team environment, you are known as the 'go to person' when it comes to finding creative solutions to client problems.

The 'Supporting Director'

If your style pairing is primary Director with secondary Supporter, then you are a rare individual indeed. Very few people have this style group pairing; however, those who do combine the qualities of *persistence* and *determination* with the Director's *competitive resolve,* resulting in people who, once they sink their teeth into a goal or task, will refuse to give up until the goal has been realized or the task completed. Sometimes referred to as human 'pit bulls' Jack Nicklaus,

Serena Williams, and Raphael Nadal are believed to share this combination profile.

In a team environment, you are the 'go to person' when something needs to get done and nobody else has the intestinal fortitude to carry it through to completion.

The 'Analyzing Director'

If your style pairing is primary Director and secondary Analyzer, you're known to combine the qualities of *precision* and *accuracy* with *competitiveness* and *directness*. Dick Cheney and Hillary Clinton, in their public persona, appear to share this 'calculating' combination. If this is your style pairing then you are known for your willingness to take direct action when there is little or no precedence set. In a team environment, you're the 'go to person' when it comes time to making and enforcing unpopular decisions.

If you have a Director engagement style, recognize that you bring uniquely specific strengths to your profession and value to your team. Ensure that you direct your work efforts toward those activities that are supported by your naturally occurring behavioral assets.

ASSESSMENT ACTION PLAN

INSIGHTS:

Know that the client engagement experience accelerates when you recognize the inherent strengths and limitations of your Director style and align your business accordingly.

SKILLS:

Apply your insights into engagement styles to help you structure your business activities to build on the strength of your directing nature.

> *"Every day above ground is a great day!"*
> – Tony Montana

I'M TOTALLY A 'CONNECTOR'

Can you talk your way out of just about any situation? Do you sometimes even surprise yourself with your *gift of the gab*? Do you love to share your opinion with others and find yourself quick to fill a conversational void? Do you often forget the name of the person whom you were just introduced to and recover with a generic name like 'Buddy' or 'Pal'? These are some of the characteristics that define this style group.

Connectors prefer to be engaged in activities that involve the participation of others in a social environment. Let's look at the behavioral assets and liabilities of Connectors.

Behavioral assets of Connectors include the ability to:

- ☺ Inspire others to take action
- ☺ Develop relationships easily
- ☺ Express service offerings with enthusiasm
- ☺ Make favorable first impressions
- ☺ Communicate in an engaging and interactive manner

Connectors accelerate their success by their naturally occurring skills during each of the three phases of the Gap Analysis Client Engagement Model©:

> During the ASSESSMENT phase, Connectors are naturally skilled at breaking the ice and building rapport. They have the ability to talk to anyone on

any topic in any place at any time. They are also gifted at asking the right questions to find commonality and develop the relationship.

During the PRESENTATION phase, Connectors are effective at communicating with confidence and enthusiasm. They are in their element when presenting their product or service offering to the market. They're also known for communicating with an engaging and dynamic vocal tone that is particularly pleasing to other members of this style group.

During the NEGOTIATION phase, Connectors negotiate with an attitude of positive expectancy. They are *open, optimistic,* and *enthusiastic.* You'll often hear encouraging phrases such as *"Let's do this," "We'll figure something out," "Don't worry about it," "I'm on it,"* and the infamous *"TRUST ME!"* They have a knack for keeping things light even when the negotiation gets heavy.

Connectors are especially effective when engaged in activities that align with their naturally outgoing engagement style.

ASSESSMENT TIP:

Connectors are especially effective when engaged in activities that align with their naturally outgoing engagement style.

Just as Connectors have naturally occurring behavioral

assets that accelerate their success, so too do they have behavioral liabilities that can hinder their success. These include a tendency to:

- Behave impulsively at times
- Lack direction and focus
- Neglect to ask for a commitment (for fear of rejection)
- Be inattentive to details
- Use time ineffectively

There are three Connector style group pairings. They include:

The 'Directing Connector'

If your style pairing is primary Connector with secondary Director, then you are known as a 'Directing Connector'. This style group pairing combines *assertiveness* and *competitiveness* with *friendliness* and *persuasion*. It is the most common pairing within this profile group. John F. Kennedy, Oprah Winfrey, and Barack Obama are all believed to share this pairing. If this is your style pairing then your greatest behavioral asset is your ability to initiate contact with people and inspire them to take action.

In a team environment you are the 'go to person' when it comes time to *opening doors, engaging others* and *inspiring action*.

The 'Supporting Connector'

If your style pairing is primary Connector with secondary Supporter, then you are known as the 'Supporting Connector'. Ellen Degeneres, Jimmy Fallon, and *Morning Express* anchor Robin Meade are believed to be members of this profile group. If this is your profile, you are known for being naturally gifted at communicating ideas and developing lasting relationships. This style group pairing combines *deliberateness* and *dependability* with *friendliness* and *persuasion*.

In a team environment you are the 'go to person' when it comes time to networking and managing on-going relationships.

The 'Analyzing Connector'

If your style pairing is primary Connector and secondary Analyzer you are known as the 'Analyzing Connector'. This style group pairing combines an attention to *detail* and *logic* with *friendliness* and *persuasion*. Many business strategists and medical equipment consultants share this behavioral pairing. If this is your engagement style then you have a natural ability to communicate complex ideas with accuracy and comprehensiveness.

In a team environment you are the 'go to person' when it comes time to motivating people to act on a technical or complex proposal.

If you have either of these 'Connector' engagement style pairings recognize that you bring uniquely specific strengths to your profession and value to your team. Ensure that you direct your work efforts toward those activities that are supported by your naturally occurring behavioral assets.

ASSESSMENT ACTION PLAN

o—— INSIGHTS:

Know that the client engagement experience accelerates when you recognize the inherent strengths and limitations of your 'Connector' style and align your business accordingly.

o—— SKILLS:

Apply your insights into engagement styles to help you structure your business activities build on the strength of your connecting nature.

> *"Slow down you move too fast,*
> *you've got to make the morning last."*
> – Paul Simon

I Feel I'm a 'Supporter'

Do you hate to be rushed into making a decision? Do you resist change and favor the status quo? Are you better one-on-one than in a group setting? Are you a better listener than you are a talker? When a friend gets cut, do you start to bleed? Are you extremely loyal to your family members, close friends, and the company that employs you? These are some of the characteristics that define this style group.

Supporters prefer performing predictable work in a stable social environment. Let's look at the behavioral assets and liabilities of Supporters.

Behavioral assets of Supporters include the ability to:

- ☺ Listen attentively and empathetically
- ☺ Remain loyal to people, teams, and companies
- ☺ Stabilize excited people (ie Connectors)
- ☺ Specialize in specific tasks or projects
- ☺ Remain poised and patient, even when under pressure

Supporters accelerate their success by their naturally occurring strengths in each of the three phases of the Gap Analysis Client Engagement Model©:

> During the ASSESSMENT phase, Supporters are gifted in the art of active listening. In fact, they are the best listeners of all four style groups, hearing both

verbal and non-verbal messages. They are also known for their empathy skills, which leaves clients feeling heard, understood, respected, and appreciated.

During the PRESENTATION phase, Supporters are effective at keeping things conversational. They have a very low-pressure sales approach that places the client's needs ahead of their own. As a result they build trust easily.

During the NEGOTIATION phase, Supporters are efficient at generating fair solutions. They will not sacrifice a relationship to achieve a one-sided outcome. They are naturally very collaborative and would rather join forces than oppose them. Supporters are also very skilled at tuning into subtle, non-verbal communication and interpreting its meaning.

Supporters are especially effective when engaged in activities that align with their naturally patient engagement style.

ASSESSMENT TIP:

Supporters are especially effective when engaged in activities that align with their naturally patient engagement style.

Just as Supporters have naturally occurring behavioral assets that accelerate their success, so too do they have behavioral liabilities that can hinder their success. These include a tendency to:

- Resist personal and professional change
- Harbor grudges toward others
- Fail to question the status quo
- Fail to be proactive when the situation demands it
- Be unwilling to confront others face to face

Supporters are reluctant to step out of their comfort zone and embrace changes within their business environment. They are more comfortable in places, and with people, that have proven to be safe, reliable and trustworthy.

There are three Supporter style group pairings. They include:

The 'Directing Supporter'

If your style pairing is primary Supporter with secondary Director, then you are often referred to as the 'Directing Supporter'. Your greatest asset is your ability to apply your natural tenacity toward task completion or goal attainment. This behavioral pairing combines *assertiveness* and *directness* with *deliberateness* and *dependability*. Michael Jordan, Wayne Gretzky, and Roger Federer are believed to share this behavioral pairing.

In a team environment you are known as the 'go to person' when it comes to applying tenacious efforts to achieve a specific and goal directed outcome, like becoming the number one basketball, hockey, or tennis player in the world.

The 'Connecting Supporter'

If your style pairing is primary Supporter with secondary Connector you are known as the 'Connecting Supporter'. This behavioral pairing combines *friendliness* and *persuasiveness* with *deliberateness* and *dependability*. If this is your profile you are an effective listener and people trust that you will do what you say. People like Carrie Underwood, Tom Hanks, and Jennifer Aniston are thought to be members of this style group.

In a team environment you are known as the 'go to person' when the team needs to establish trust and manage the on-going client relationship.

The 'Analyzing Supporter'
This style pairing combines an adherence to *policy* and *procedure* with the qualities of *dependability* and *deliberateness*. The medical, dental and legal professions are well represented by members of this style group. Well-known airline pilot Chelsea "Sully" Sullenberger, who safely and calmly landed an Airbus A320 onto the Hudson River, is believed to have this style group pairing. If this is your pairing as well, you are naturally effective at performing to a consistent and acceptable work standard, even in the face of challenging circumstances.

In a team environment you are the 'go to person' when it comes time to setting the team up with systems for accountability.

If you have either of these Supporter engagement styles, recognize that you bring uniquely specific strengths to your profession and value to your team. Ensure that you direct your work efforts toward those activities that are supported by your naturally occurring engagement strengths.

ASSESSMENT ACTION PLAN

○── INSIGHTS:

Know that the client engagement experience accelerates when you recognize the inherent strengths and limitations of your Supporter style and align your business accordingly.

○── SKILLS:

Apply your insights into engagement styles to help you structure your business to build on the strengths of your supporting nature.

> *"Beware of the person who can't be bothered by the details."*
> – William Feather

I THINK I'M AN 'ANALYZER'

Do you get frustrated with those who buck policy or bypass procedure? Do you like to double-check your work to ensure accuracy? Do you require a lot of information before you make a purchase decision and sometimes obsess over the details? When you buy electronics, do you fill out the warranty cards or purchase the extended warranty to protect your investment? Are you adamant about paying your bills on time at the end of every month? These are some characteristics that define this style group.

Analyzers prefer working toward task completion on activities related to your subject matter expertise. Let's look at the behavioral assets and liabilities of an Analyzer success partner.

Behavioral assets of an Analyzer include the ability to:

- ☺ Follow policy and procedure
- ☺ Communicate in a diplomatic manner
- ☺ Ensure standards are met
- ☺ Operate in a controlled environment
- ☺ Deliver as promised

Analyzers accelerate their success by applying their natural occurring strengths in each of the three phases of the Gap Analysis Client Engagement Model©:

During the ASSESSMENT phase, Analyzers are naturally skilled at listening for factual content. They are very methodical in their approach to uncover their client's needs and are known for their ability to communicate with patience and diplomacy. Unlike Supporters, who are *empathetic* listeners, Analyzers are *attentive* listeners, skilled in the art of hearing and interpreting relevant factual data.

During the PRESENTATION phase, Analyzers are effective at delivering thorough and well-structured presentations. Although not known for their engaging delivery style or charismatic presence, they are extremely competent when presenting on topics of their expertise.

During the NEGOTIATION phase, Analyzers are highly skilled at uncovering evidence to support their negotiating position. They are accurate and thorough in their research and diligence drafting enforceable contracts. Analyzers don't like to make mistakes so they dot all their 'i's' and cross all their 't's'. When encountering resistance they'll remain non-confrontational, preferring to work through problems using logic and reason as their guide.

Analyzers are especially effective when engaged in activities that align with their naturally analytical engagement style.

Just as Analyzers have naturally occurring behavioral assets that accelerate their success, so too do they have behavioral liabilities that can hinder their success. These include a tendency to:

- Yield a position to avoid confrontation
- Dismiss ideas that are not supported by logic

- Get bogged down in excessive detail
- Fail to take action if no precedence is set
- Get defensive when their findings are questioned

There are three Analyzer style group pairings. They include:

The 'Directing Analyzer'

If your style pairing is primary Analyzer with secondary Director then you are known as the 'Directing Analyzer'. This style group pairing blends the qualities of *assertiveness* and *directness* with a *logical* and *systematic* nature. Your greatest asset is your ability to apply standards, rules, and systems and ensure they are followed. Bill Gates, Mark Zuckerberg, and the late Steve Jobs are thought to share this engagement style.

In a team environment you are known as the 'go to person' when it comes to establishing systems and ensuring full compliance.

The 'Connecting Analyzer'

If your style pairing is primary Analyzer with secondary Connector then you are someone who is *accurate, detailed and compliant* as well as *outgoing, gregarious,* and *charming*. It is the behavioral equivalent of a tax auditor with a great sense of humor. Although somewhat rare, those who do share this style group pairing are affectionately referred to as a 'Connecting Analyzer'. If this is you then you're known to have a naturally strong ability to promote conceptual ideas using logic and reason.

In a team environment you are the 'go to person' when it comes to managing people operating in a complex environment.

The 'Supporting Analyzer'

If your profile is primarily Analyzer and secondary Supporter then you have a strong ability to maintain high standards and follow policy and procedures. This behavioral pairing combines *deliberateness* and *consistency* with *accuracy* and *logic*. Individuals sharing this engagement style are thought to include John McCain, Al Gore, and environmental steward David Suzuki.

In a team environment you are the 'go to person' when it comes time to communicating the technical aspects of a sophisticated product/ service offering.

If you have either of these Analyzer engagement styles, recognize that you bring uniquely specific strengths to your profession and value to your team. Ensure that you direct your work efforts toward those activities that are supported by your naturally occurring behavioral strengths.

ASSESSMENT ACTION PLAN

INSIGHTS:

Know that the client engagement experience accelerates when you recognize the inherent strengths and limitations of your Analyzer style and align your business accordingly.

SKILLS:

Apply your insights into engagement styles to help you structure your business to build on the strengths of your analyzing nature.

The Assessment Phase

~Chapter Two~
Assessing Your Client's Engagement Style

Accelerate your professional success by recognizing your client's preferred style of engagement.

"We don't see things as they are; we see things as we are."
– Anais Nin

> *"A client's 'engagement style' can easily be identified if you're willing to look for the signs."*
> – Gerald Gordon Clerx

TUNING IN TO YOUR CLIENT

Just as a person's engagement style impacts how she sells, so too does it impact how she prefers to buy. Knowing a client's engagement style is imperative if you are to design and deliver a presentation that aligns accordingly.

ASSESSMENT TIP:

Knowing a client's engagement style is imperative if you are to design and deliver a presentation that aligns accordingly.

Assessing a client's engagement style is not as difficult as you might think. In fact, behavioral clues are visible for all to see; however, they will only have meaning for those who know how to interpret its meaning. When you get good at this you can assess profiles in a very short period of time, sometimes instantly.

A client's engagement style will provide you with insights into exactly what he or she needs to *see, hear*, and *experience* to fully support a favorable buying decision. The quickest way to identify a client's style is to observe *verbal, vocal,* and *visual* communication patterns, known as 'style identifiers':

Style Identifier - Verbal

When observing verbal patterns, pay attention to the types of *words* and *phrases* being used as well as the types of *questions* asked. Different styles rely more heavily on certain words and ask different questions designed to elicit specific types of information.

ASSESSMENT TIP:

When observing verbal patterns, pay attention to the types of *words* and *phrases* being used as well as the *questions* asked.

Style Identifier - Vocal

When observing vocal communication patterns, pay attention to your client's *pace, tone,* and *volume.*

Your client's vocal patterns will help you narrow down his/ her engagement style through a process of elimination. For instance: two style groups speak quicker than the norm and two slower; two use a more businesslike tone and two a more casual tone; two speak at a louder volume and two softer.

Style Identifier - Visual

When observing visual patterns, focus in on *body posture, hand gestures,* and *facial expressions.* It is estimated that body language accounts for 57 percent of the communicated message, so pay close attention to what is being conveyed visually.

ASSESSMENT TIP:

It is estimated that body language accounts for 57 percent of the communicated message.

The reason why most success partners fail to recognize their client's engagement style is because they're being 'self-centric' rather than 'client-centric' in their behavior. They're more concerned with what they're saying and how they're appearing than they are on the communication nuances of their client.

When assessing your client's engagement style, however, be sure to base your assessment on more than just one clue. Use a 'clustering technique' by making multiple observations over a period of a few minutes, to ensure the greatest degree of accuracy.

The next time you meet a new client, tune in verbally by listening to the *words* and *phrases* used and the types of *questions* asked. Tune in vocally to *tone, pace,* and *volume* and finally tune in visually by observing *body posture, hand gestures,* and *facial expressions.* A lot can be learned by paying attention to your client's communication patterns.

But keep in mind, observation is only the first step; interpretation is the second. In the following four acceleration strategies, you'll learn how to identify each of the four engagement styles by interpreting the communication patterns associated with each one.

ASSESSMENT ACTION PLAN

INSIGHTS:

Know that the client engagement experience accelerates when you seek to determine the engagement style of your client.

SKILLS:

Apply a clustering technique to focus on what your client is saying (verbal) and how she is saying it (vocal and visual) to identify his/ her style.

RESOURCES:

Refer to the *Client Assessment Tool* to determine your client's engagement style. Go to www.theGAPanalysis.com and click on 'Resources' page to learn more.

> *"Do not go where the path may lead,
> go instead where there is no path and leave a trail."*
> – Ralph Waldo Emerson

HOW TO RECOGNIZE 'DIRECTORS'

If you've ever had a client interrupt your presentation by asking *"What's the bottom line?"* or by saying *"Cut to the chase,"* or by tapping fingers when wanting you to pick up the pace? If you've ever had a client take your proposal from your hands and turn straight to the last page to check out how much it's going to cost or how much he stands to make in the transaction then you've been in the presence of a Director client.

Remember, Directors are *actively paced* and *task focused*, which means they like to move quickly toward a specific and tangible result.

Spotting a Director is an easy thing to do if you can identify their verbal, vocal and visual communication patterns:

Director - Verbal Identifiers

Let's start with the words and phrases that you'll hear expressed more frequently by members of this profile group. Words such *as success, results, priority access, quickly, outcome, driven, aggressive, leadership, top dollar, top producer, assert,* and *overcome* are all prominent in the Director vocabulary. Some of their other common phrases include:

Get to the point!
You've got to be kidding me!

Quit wasting my time!
Let's get down to business!
Skip the small talk!
and, in Donald Trump's case, *YOU'RE FIRED!*

A client's engagement style can also be determined by listening to the types of questions asked. Since Directors *fear failure* and *desire quick results*, the bulk of their questions will seek to either alleviate their fears or confirm the realization of their desires. For example, during the ASSESSMENT phase a Director client might ask:
How long is this going to take?
What do you have for me?
What's your fee and how do you justify it?
What is the upside potential?
How quickly can you turn this around?

A Director's questions are intended to elicit the essential information required to make a quick decision leading to a tangible outcome.

Director - Vocal Identifiers

A Director client can also be recognized by his/ her vocal *pace*, *tone*, and *volume*.

Since they are in the active behavior quadrant, their vocal *pace* moves along at a faster clip when compared to the norm. They don't necessarily speak quicker but they do get to the point quicker, as reflected in their bottom line-oriented questioning style.

Vocally, Directors have a *tone* that is more businesslike and matter-of-fact than the norm. Indeed, they are the most matter-of-fact and businesslike of all four engagement styles.

The *volume* of their voice covers a wide dynamic range, from quiet and controlled to loud and assertive. When frustrated, the Directors vocal *volume* can rise sharply with little or no warning.

Director – Visual Identifiers

Directors are easy to see, as well. Visually their body posture is more rigid than the other styles. They stand and sit in a more upright position and lean in when expressing their opinions or showing interest in your product/ service offering.

Their more assertive nature can also be observed in the way they point their index finger toward those things that interest them and the way they pound their index finger into the table to ensure their point is made. Peaking the fingertips in an *"I'm in control here"* way is another classic Director hand gesture. While other style groups use more expansive and/ or open-palmed hand gestures, Director gesturing is more directional and out in front.

A handshake from a Director client is another strong clue. It will almost always involve a firm grip accompanied by direct eye contact. In some cases you'll receive a handshake that begins vertically and ends up with them turning your hand into a horizontal position, with theirs on top. This is a subtle way in which some Directors test your response to assertive behavior. If they encounter physical resistance during the greeting, they'll know to expect verbal resistance during the negotiation.

Facial expressions account for the balance of behavioral identifiers. The Directors forehead often supports a furrowed brow, especially when questioning the source of your information. The eyes are usually fixed in an intense gaze and smiles are not easily forthcoming. If a smile is elicited during the sales cycle, it will likely be short-lived, so as not to encourage small talk or suggest conviviality.

Another way to obtain clues into your client's

engagement style is by noticing their workplace. A Directors work environment is often bold, clean, and efficient and the office walls adorned with awards to showcase personal accomplishments.

The Directors three favorite colors are black, dark black, and midnight black. Actually it's black, navy, and charcoal grey, which are the traditional power colors in our society. The vast majority of automobiles targeted toward this buyer group come in these three primary color choices. If this profile group had a theme song it would be 'I Did It My Way', sung by the King of all Directors, Frank Sinatra.

Director clients are easy to spot, straight to the point, and quick to engage with success partners who understand their unique needs and adapt accordingly.

ASSESSMENT TIP:

Director clients are easy to spot and quick to partner with success partners who understand their unique needs and adapt accordingly.

When you first meet with a prospective client, pay close attention to their engagement style. Knowing the client's style is an important piece of the client engagement cycle because, as you will discover in Chapter Five, presenting your product offering or service solution to a Director client looks and sounds nothing like delivering a presentation to other engagement styles.

ASSESSMENT ACTION PLAN

INSIGHTS:

Know that the client engagement experience accelerates when you recognize a Director client and tailor the engagement experience accordingly.

SKILLS:

Apply observation skills to detect if your client is a Director by tuning into:

- Language that reflects an *active pace* and *task focus*.

- Vocal qualities that include a *faster pace*, *business tone*, and *louder volume*.

- Body language that includes an *erect posture*, *assertive hand gestures,* and more *intense facial expressions*.

> *"I don't like myself ... I'm crazy about myself"*
> – Mae West

How to Recognize 'Connectors'

If you've ever met a client who loved to talk, or if you've ever shown up late for an appointment and your client showed up later, or if you've ever met someone who gave you a hearty double-handed, triple-pumping handshake accompanied by a broad, friendly grin then you've been in the presence of a Connector client.

Connectors are *actively paced* and *socially focused*, which means they like to move enthusiastically toward the development of the relationship. The product/ service outcome is almost secondary to the engagement process.

Here are some of the *verbal*, *vocal*, and *visual* identifiers of the Connector client:

Verbal Identifiers

Verbal identifiers include words and phrases that are more descriptive and colorful by nature. Ask a Connector how she is doing and you will likely get a response such as *I'm excellent, Couldn't be better*! or perhaps even *Outstanding*! The responses of *I'm fine* or *I'm OK* are not common amongst Connectors, even if they are feeling under the weather. Some favored phrases reflective of this group's enthusiastic and optimistic nature include:

No worries!
Not a problem!
Great to finally meet you!
How the heck are you!

Now where were we?
Where did the day go? And
Sorry I'm late! (Connectors have a far more elastic concept of time than the other style groups)

The greatest fear of the Connector is *loss of influence*, and the greatest desire is for *recognition and acceptance*. These two underlying motivators are reflected in the often personally directed questions a Connector client may ask you, which might include:
So how long have you been in the business?
How do you like the business?
*Which one of these is **your** favorite?*
*What do **you** recommend we should do?*
Are you doing anything later this week?

It's important to note that Connectors are relationship driven, so they inherently seek to connect with others whenever and wherever the opportunity avails itself. In many cases, short-term professional partnerships can develop into long-term personal friendships.

Vocal Identifiers
Now let's shift to vocal identifiers, beginning with *pace*. Of all four engagement styles, Connectors speak the fastest. In some cases they'll speak before fully thinking through the consequences of their words. *"I can't believe I just said that,"* or *"Did I just say that out loud?"* are classic recovery phrases for the Connector. Virtually all feet ending up in the mouths of their owner belong to members of this particular style group.

Regarding vocal *tone*, Connectors are far less businesslike than their Director counterparts. Rather than *"Let's get down to business,"* it's more like *"Tell me a little about yourself*" or better yet, "*Let me tell you a little about myself.*"

Vocal *volume* for Connectors is, on average, louder than the norm. Other style groups may find this characteristic to be a source of annoyance, especially the less gregarious Supporter and Analyzer style groups.

Visual Identifiers

Visually, Connectors are easy to spot. Their enthusiastic persona is often expressed through brighter colors and trendier clothes adorned with more plentiful accessories. Favored colors include red, yellow and other more cheerful hues.

A Connectors body language is loose and open and they tend to lean toward those things of interest to them. They get closer, quicker than other engagement styles, and they are far more comfortable sharing their space, especially within their style group. Physical contact is far more prevalent between members of this profile group. Receiving a touch to the top of the hand or back of the elbow is not uncommon while engaged in conversation with the Connector.

Their hand gestures are more expansive and more animated than most others. Whereas Directors tend to limit their gestures to a 45-degree range directly in front, Connectors express themselves with a full 180-degree range of motion. They'll often exaggerate their gestures to make a point (i.e. the size of the fish actually caught is rarely the size of the fish they claim they caught).

Receiving a handshake from a Connector can also be a unique experience, especially if you are not familiar with this engagement style. A double-pumping shake accompanied by a broad smile and enthusiastic greeting is the norm. Heck, you may even receive the infamous double-handed, double-pumping handshake, which indicates of a high level of personal acceptance.

However, be wary of the double-handed, *triple-pumping* handshake. If you get one of these from a Connector client leave the area immediately—as he or she likely has bigger plans for you.

Connectors are, by far, the most animated of all four styles. Broader smiles and more extreme reactions are the norm. When listening, they nod their head in an enthusiastic and encouraging way (even if they haven't the foggiest idea of what you're talking about). This group can give the outward appearance of being fully engrossed in your story while mentally sipping a margarita on some sunny tropical beach.

The Connector's office environment is brighter and bolder than the other style groups; however, it will likely appear to be a little on the chaotic side. Photographs and pictures are often self-directed, showcasing unique personal experiences or adventures. Their office is set up to be more conducive for socializing than for work, and the desk will most likely be facing the door to facilitate dialogue with passers by.

If the Connector had a theme song, it would be 'Don't Worry, Be Happy'. These lyrics represent their basic life philosophy. Ahh, Connectors—you've got to love them! I mean that seriously, **you've got to**. It's the expectation Connectors have from all their acquaintances, personal or professional.

Connectors are easy to spot and eager to engage with success partners who understand their unique needs and adapt accordingly.

ASSESSMENT TIP:

Connectors are easy to spot, and eager to partner with success partners who understand their unique needs and adapt accordingly.

The client engagement experience accelerates when success partners recognize a Connector client and tailor the engagement experience accordingly.

As you'll discover in Chapter Five; presenting your product offering or service solution to a Connector client looks and sounds nothing like delivering a presentation to other engagement styles.

ASSESSMENT ACTION PLAN

INSIGHTS:

Know that the client engagement experience accelerates when you recognize a Connector client and tailor the engagement experience accordingly.

SKILLS:

Apply observation skills to detect if your client is a Connector by tuning into:

- Language that reflects an *active pace* and *social focus*.

- Vocal qualities that include a *faster pace, friendlier tone*, and *louder volume*.

- Body language that includes a more *casual posture* with *animated gestures* and *facial expressions*.

> "I know God will not give me anything I can't handle. I just wish He didn't trust me so much."
> – Mother Teresa

How to Recognize 'Supporters'

If you've ever had a client greet you with a warm smile and a gentle handshake and follow up by asking genuine questions and listening intently to your responses then you've interacted with a Supporter client.

Supporters are *passively paced* and *socially focused*, which means that they move deliberately toward an understanding of people and processes. Spotting them is an easy thing to do if you know the *verbal*, *vocal*, and *visual* clues offered up by this engagement style.

Verbal Identifiers

Verbally, Supporters communicate with a strong reliance on words such as *together*, *we've*, and *let's*. It's called the language of collaboration and they speak it fluently. Commonly used Supporter phrases include:
That seems fair.
I'll go along with that.
It is a pleasure to meet you.
Thank you so much for coming.
Wouldn't you agree?
I'm just looking, thank you.

Now reflect on these phrases for a moment. You just won't hear these statements made by a Director client.

The Supporters greatest fear is *loss of stability*, and his/

her great desire is for *safety and security*; therefore the questions asked will reflect these two underlying motivators. During the ASSESSMENT phase, a Supporter client might ask:

Who will be involved in this sale or project?
What are their respective roles?
Who is my contact person?
Can you provide me some timelines?
Who else have you worked with?
Do you have any references?
Can I return it if I am not happy?
Do you guarantee your work?

Vocal Identifiers

Vocally, Supporters speak at a slower and more *deliberate pace* than the norm. They are in no hurry and their vocal pace reflects this more relaxed conversational style.

Regarding vocal *tone*, the Supporter is less businesslike than the Director but more businesslike than the Connector.

A Supporter's vocal *volume* is much softer than the previous two engagement styles. They exhibit more patience than others, and their pauses are longer as they give more thought-*full* consideration to their responses.

Visual Identifiers

Visually, Supporters have a more relaxed posture. They spend more time in a listening mode and will keep their distance until trust has been established. You can often observe them leaning back, reflecting upon the information presented.

Their hand gestures are gentler and less expansive than the Directors and Connectors. Instead of pointing gestures, they rely more on open-palmed and rolling hand gestures.

A Supporter's handshake is warm, friendly, and the least

firm of the four profile groups overall. In some cases the hand is extended without any firmness to their grip whatsoever (note: this can also reflect a culturally inherited mannerism). Supporters do not feel the need to deliver an assertive or overly enthusiastic greeting. It's not a sincere reflection of who they are.

Facial expressions during initial greetings can best be described as warm and inviting. They convey acceptance with a relaxed smile and reassuring eyes. Be assured, however, that their pleasant demeanor will shift if they feel threatened or mislead.

The Supporter dresses more for comfort than for prestige or impact. Sweaters, loose-fitting clothes, and soft-soled shoes are more the norm for this style group. This is not to say that they will always be casually attired, it's just more within their comfort zone.

Their office will also reflect their desire for comfort with images of family and loved ones displayed throughout. Their personal space will have a cozier and warmer feel than the other style groups, with preferred colors being earth tones such as white, beige, and greens.

If the Supporter had a theme song it would be, 'That's What Friends Are For'; after all, the Supporters identity is strongly linked to the quality of his or her personal and professional relationships.

Supporter clients are easy to spot and secure in engaging with success partners who understand their unique needs and adapt accordingly.

ASSESSMENT TIP:

Supporter clients are easy to spot and

secure in partnering with success partners who understand their unique needs and adapt accordingly.

The client engagement experience accelerates when success partners recognize a Supporter client and tailor the engagement experience accordingly.

As you'll discover in Chapter Five, presenting your product offering or service solution to a Supporter client looks and sounds nothing like presenting to other engagement styles.

ASSESSMENT ACTION PLAN

○━ INSIGHTS:

Know that the client engagement experience accelerates when you recognize a Supporter client and tailor the engagement experience accordingly.

○━ SKILLS:

Apply observation skills to detect if your client is a Supporter by tuning into:

- Language that reflects a *passive pace* and *social focus*.

- Vocal qualities that include a *slower pace, friendlier tone* and *softer volume*.

- Body language that includes a *relaxed posture, softer hand gestures*, and *warmer facial expressions*.

> *"Facts are stubborn things."*
> – Ronald Reagan

HOW TO RECOGNIZE 'ANALYZERS'

If you've ever had a client ask more than the usual amount of questions and require a lot of evidence to support a buying decision, or if the client spoke painfully slow by your standards, or had a greater depth and breadth of knowledge of your competitors' offering than you did, then you've interacted with an Analyzer.

Analyzers are *passively paced* and *task focused*, which means they move methodically toward a comprehensive understanding of the situation. Spotting an Analyzer is an easy thing to do if you know the *verbal*, *vocal*, and *visual* clues offered up by clients with this engagement style.

Verbal Identifiers

Analyzers are heavily reliant on words that are both qualitative and quantitative. Words like; *assessment, comprehensive, historical analysis, proof, assurances,* and *guarantees* are frequently relied upon to communicate ideas and opinions. Common Analyzer phrases include:

It seems to me.
That sounds <u>reasonable</u>.
I'll <u>consider</u> that.
Let me <u>think</u> it over.
Leave it with me.

Consider the words that are underlined: *reasonable* (reason able), *consider* and *think*. This is the left-brained and linear dialogue of the Analyzer client, and it is as distinct a language as English is from French.

Remember, the Analyzers greatest fear is *making a mistake*, and his/ her greatest desire is for *full and accurate disclosure*. These underlying motivators are evidenced by the types of questions Analyzers ask, which are intended to gather the information necessary to support their logical decision-making needs.

During your interaction with an Analyzer, he or she might ask:

How did you arrive at these figures?
Is your commission negotiable?
Why is your competitor 30% cheaper than you are?
What are the operating costs of this product?
Where is this product manufactured?
Do you have any updated spec sheets?
Are you prepared to put up any assurances or guarantees?

Vocal Identifiers

Analyzers vocal *pace* matches their information processing preference, which tends to be much slower than the norm. They are not quick to render decisions, which can be a great source of frustration for the faster paced Directors and Connectors.

Their vocal *tone* is the most formal of all engagement styles and can be recognized by a conservative, businesslike, and often monotone quality. Listening to an Analyzer talk for a long period of time is a real test to the attention span of the other three engagement styles.

Their vocal *volume* is lower than the norm and in some cases you may have to lean in and strain to hear their words.

Visual Identifiers

The body posture of the Analyzer is less open than the more social Connectors and Supporters. In a sales environment the Analyzer prefers to keep a distance, while carefully considering the information being presented.

Their hand gestures are far less expansive or expressive than the other style groups, with arms remaining tighter to their bodies. Their handshake, by comparison, is conservative and can be recognized by a firm grip without the intense and enduring eye contact of the Director.

Analyzers facial expressions are the least animated of the four engagement styles.

Physically, the appearance of the Analyzer is more conservative than the other style groups. Rather than dressing for impact, trend consciousness or comfort, they dress to reflect professionalism.

You can expect their office environment to be tidy and symmetrical. Pictures will be hung with precision and credentials will be prominently displayed as a show of professional competence. Preferred colors include the more conservative tones of browns, navy blues, and grey.

Analyzers are detail-oriented and confident in engaging with success partners who understand their unique needs and adapt accordingly.

ASSESSMENT TIP:

Analyzers are detail-oriented and confident in engaging with success partners who understand their unique needs and adapt accordingly.

As you'll discover in Chapter Five; presenting your

product offering or service solution to an Analyzer client looks and sounds nothing like delivering a presentation to the other buyer profiles.

So there you have it: the verbal, vocal, and visual identifiers of the four profile groups. By following these guidelines, you should be able to identify the buyer profile of your next client within the first few minutes of your initial meeting.

However, keep in mind that knowing your client's engagement style is only one piece of a two-piece puzzle. In PART II of this book, you'll discover how to take this client awareness and use it to shape your presentation and tailor its delivery. You'll learn what to say and why, and how to say it in a way that supports the client's unique decision-making needs.

ASSESSMENT ACTION PLAN

INSIGHTS:

Know that the client engagement experience accelerates when you recognize an Analyzer client and tailor the engagement experience accordingly.

SKILLS:

Apply observation skills to detect if your client is an Analyzer by tuning into:

- Language that reflects a *passive pace* and *task focus*.

- Vocal qualities that includes a *slower pace*, *businesslike tone* and *softer volume*.

- Body language that includes a more *defensive posture*, *less animated gestures*, and *more reserved facial expressions*.

The Assessment Phase

~Chapter Three~
Assessing Your Client's Gap

Accelerate your professional success by isolating your client's current reality situation and desired reality outcome.

"Seek first to understand, then to be understood."
– Stephen Covey

> *"If your clients don't have confidence in your assessment of their problem, they won't have confidence in your solution."*
> – Gerald Gordon Clerx

SEEK FIRST TO UNDERSTAND

In Chapter Two I introduced you to an assessment strategy to help you identify the engagement style of your client.

In addition to profiling your client, the other purpose of the ASSESSMENT phase is to isolate the gap between where your client is and where he/ she wants to be.

ASSESSMENT TIP:

The other purpose of the ASSESSMENT phase is to isolate the gap between your client's current situation and desired outcome.

These reference points form the foundation upon which every product presentation or service proposal is built—a road map, if you will, complete with a clearly defined departure point and arrival destination. Once these are known, your role is to simply bridge that gap with the best product/ service solution available.

As a success-minded success partner, your primary

objective should be to fully and accurately uncover your client's gap. Depending on the type of product you sell or service you promote, there could be up to fifty pieces of information required to accurately establish your client's gap.

ASSESSMENT TIP:

Depending on the type of product you sell or service you promote, there could be up to fifty pieces of information required to accurately establish your client's gap.

Now I'm not suggesting that you corner a client and fire off fifty high velocity questions; however, I am suggesting that you engage them in a fact-finding dialogue to gather as much information as possible before you make your recommendations.

Also bear in mind that the questioning approach you employ should be a reflection of your client's engagement style.

Let's stop for a minute and test your styles knowledge here. Which two style groups will not tolerate a lengthy questioning strategy? .... You'd be right if you identified the Directors and Connectors. The Directors don't have the time and the Connectors don't have the attention span. Now don't get me wrong, you'll still require the information; however, you might have to bridge the information gaps via a third party source or some on-line research.

On the other hand, Supporters and Analyzers will respond far more favorably to a comprehensive questioning strategy. Why? Because they're in no hurry to make a decision! In fact, their respective key motivators—a *desire* for safety and a *fear* of making a mistake—both align favorably with a success partner who takes the time up front to ask a series of questions that ensure a safe and mistake-free outcome.

An inconclusive assessment causes everyone to lose. You lose, your client loses, and so too does anyone else who has time or money invested in the transaction.

On the flip side, a comprehensive assessment almost always guarantees you a successful outcome. It allows you to show fewer, more selectively defined products and it makes it easier for your client to say, *"yes"* to your recommendation. And because your client will recognize you as a competent and skilled professional, he or she will feel less inclined to request a price or fee concession as a condition of purchase.

Success partners who are attentive and empathetic listeners are in high demand and short supply.

ASSESSMENT ACTION PLAN

○── INSIGHTS:

Know that the best way to deliver a successful client engagement experience is to build it on the foundation of a conclusive assessment.

○── SKILLS:

Apply a comprehensive questioning strategy that effectively isolates your client's product or service gap.

○── RESOURCES:

Refer to the following two Acceleration Strategies as your resources to help you uncover your client's *desired reality outcome* and *current reality situation*.

> *"If you don't know where you're going,
> any road will take you there."*
> – Yogi Berra

WHERE ARE YOU GOING

The primary objective of your assessment questions is to get your client to clearly articulate a vision of a desirable outcome. Clarity of purpose is a powerful thing. When clients are clear of exactly what they want, what they want tends to show up for them. You are far better off working with clients who can describe with absolute certainty what they're looking for, because they'll be able to recognize it when you deliver it.

ASSESSMENT TIP:

**Clarity of vision is a powerful thing.
When clients are clear of exactly
what they want, what they want
tends to show up for them.**

Your client's desired reality has been fully defined when you have certainty on three decision-making criteria: *Satisfiers*, *Justifiers* and *Motivators*.

Satisfiers
Satisfiers represent what the client needs to have included

in your product or service offering. Depending on the offering, these needs could include:

- *Design needs,* which include the elements of product shape and/ or layout.
- *Material needs,* which include product construction type and texture.
- *Aesthetic needs,* which include product color and appearance.
- *Expansion needs,* which include product integration and compatibility features.
- *Functionality needs,* which include product ease of use and accessibility.
- *Economic needs,* which include product price, operating costs and maintenance costs.
- *Timing needs,* which include closing dates and delivery time frames.
- *Flexibility needs,* which include the ability to change or modify the product/ service offering.

Justifiers

Justifiers are represented by what the client needs to know to support a purchase decision. This information is necessary to support the logical side of the decision-making brain. Understanding your client's engagement style will provide you with insights into the type of information they require. Director and Analyzer profiles are highly logical and linear in their decision-making process; therefore, they'll want tangible evidence to support their purchase decision.

Director clients prefer a factual overview, while Analyzers prefer full disclosure, including all relevant facts, figures, statistics, and case studies. Connectors and Supporters are less reliant on factual evidence and instead prefer third party testimonials, which they find more personal.

Motivators

Motivators are represented by what your client needs to feel in order to support a purchase decision.

Key motivators can be elicited by asking probing questions such as, *"Why is that important to you?"* or *"What will that give you"?* The client's underlying key motivator will likely be uncovered by one of these probing questions. For instance, a need to drive a brightly colored vehicle or live in a trendy part of town might be inspired by a desire to feel more youthful or attractive to others.

Desires represent 'moving toward' motivators and accelerate favorable buying decisions. Some of the more common desire-based motivators include:

- A *desire* to grow intellectually or spiritually
- A *desire* to look better
- A *desire* to feel better
- A *desire* to feel safer
- A *desire* for more convenience
- A *desire* to save time or become more productive
- A *desire* to live longer
- A *desire* to accumulate wealth
- A *desire* to be first
- A *desire* to be understood
- A *desire* for more meaning
- A *desire* for better relationships
- A *desire* for better performance
- A *desire* for recognition and acknowledgement
- A *desire* to feel informed

ASSESSMENT TIP:

Motivators can be expressed as either *fears* or *desires*.

Fears represent 'moving away from' motivators and support buying decisions if your client believes that your product or service offering will take them away from that which they *fear*. Some of the more common *fears* that can inspire a favorable buying decision include:

- A *fear* of missing out
- A *fear* of losing
- A *fear* of change
- A *fear* of being trapped in an uncomfortable situation
- A *fear* of being rejected
- A *fear* of being judged critically
- A *fear* of not living up to another's expectation
- A *fear* of failing
- A *fear* of making a mistake
- A *fear* of dying
- A *fear* of becoming a burden to others
- A *fear* of being hurt (physically or emotionally)
- A *fear* of hurting someone else

Home security systems, prescription drugs, breath mints, dandruff control shampoos, and cosmetics are a few product offerings that have generated a lot of revenue by promising to move you away from what you *fear*.

ASSESSMENT ACTION PLAN

INSIGHTS:

Know that the client engagement experience accelerates when you generate a full understanding of the client's desired reality outcome.

SKILLS:

Apply a comprehensive questioning strategy that accurately assesses your client's *satisfiers, justifiers,* and *motivators.*

RESOURCES:

Refer to our *Gap Questioning Strategy* to assist you in isolating your client's *desired reality outcome.* Go to www.theGAPanalysis.com and click on 'Resources' page to learn more.

> *"If you don't know where you are ...*
> ***YOU'RE LOST!"***
> – Gerald Gordon Clerx

WHERE ARE YOU NOW

The secondary objective of the gap analysis is to get your client to clarify their current reality situation. The questions you ask should confirm the following current reality insights:

Financial ability
These insights establish what the client is willing to pay or able to afford. Obviously, financial ability is only relevant on larger ticket items.

Current Status
Current reality questions should also ascertain if the client needs to *upgrade, replace* or *amend* his/ her existing product or service agreement. Depending on the complexity of the offering, your *current* reality questioning strategy could include the following questions:

- *Tell me about your current product/ service provider.*
- *When does your current product lease/service agreement expire?*
- *Who else is involved in the decision-making process?*
- *What criteria will you use to make your decision?*
- *What is your time frame for this project?*
- *What are your current usage patterns?*
- *What other considerations do you have?*

Obviously, the complexity of your questioning strategy should be a reflection of the complexity of your product or service offering.

In some instances your gap analysis will confirm that your client is not a valid prospect ... in other words their desired reality outcome is not possible based on their current reality situation.

In this case, assuming they are unwilling to redefine their desired reality outcome, you may have to disengage the relationship and recommend they go elsewhere. To carry on would be futile and an unproductive use of time for all parties involved.

Summary

An effectively conducted assessment provides you with a complete understanding of the client and her product/ service gap. With these reference points known, you are in a position to move into the **second** phase of the Gap Analysis Client Engagement Model©, the PRESENTATION phase.

In the next part of this book, you'll learn how to take the information uncovered during the ASSESSMENT phase and use it to deliver the right solution in a way that aligns perfectly with the client's decision-making needs. You'll also discover a powerful whole-brain reasoning technique for structuring your message so that it *informs logically* and *inspires emotionally*. And finally, you will learn how to add impact to your message and enhance its long-term retention.

I will conclude this part of the book with a driving analogy that playfully summarizes the unique response habits of each engagement style group:

Question: What do you get when four Directors approach a four way stop sign?

Answer: **An accident!** Because they all assume the other drivers will yield to them.

Question: What do you get when four Connectors approach a four way stop sign?

Answer: **A party!** Any time you have four Connectors together you have the makings of a spontaneous party.

Question: What do you get when four Supporters approach a four way stop sign?

Answer: **Gridlock!** Because they all patiently wave the other drivers through the intersection!

Question: What do you get when four Analyzers approach a four way stop sign?

Answer: **They get out of the car, form a committee and redesign the intersection!** (Note: I'm convinced that is where the roundabout concept came from.)

ASSESSMENT ACTION PLAN

INSIGHTS:

Know that the client engagement experience accelerates when you fully and accurately uncover the client's *current reality* situation.

SKILLS:

Apply a comprehensive questioning strategy that accurately establishes your client's *current reality* situation.

RESOURCES:

Refer to our *Gap Questioning Strategy* to assist you in isolating your client's *current reality* situation. Go to www.theGAPanalysis.com and click on 'Resources' page to learn more.

Excellence in Action – ASSESSMENT

> Isadore (Izzy) Sharp, in his tenure as CEO of the Four Seasons Hotel chain was a master at the art of assessing his client's needs, even before it became fashionable to do so.
>
> The first Four Seasons hotel was built in Toronto, Ontario Canada in the early 60's. It was a rather modest hotel by current standards but it was the beginning of a hotel empire founded on the golden rule ... 'treat others as you would like to be treated'. This rule was backed by an unrelenting commitment to providing an outstanding customer experience.
>
> Exceeding customer expectations requires an acute ability to identify gaps in the first place and then bridge them with innovative product or service solutions. And there was no one better at this than Izzy Sharp.
>
> Izzy was known to have spent much of his time talking to customer's to uncover their desired reality outcomes and then evaluate them against current reality standards. Once those two reference points were known he went to work building bridges to span those gaps and deliver his customers to a superior hotel experience.
>
> In fact, he was credited with the following service 'extras' that have since become 'standards' in the hotel industry.
>
> - Shampoo bottles in all bathrooms (in the early days)
> - Bathrobes and slippers in all rooms
> - Telephones in the bathroom
> - Workout facilities in all hotels
> - Television sets in front of the treadmills and workout equipment
>
> It is well documented that Izzy would often just show up unannounced to any one of his hotels and tour it through the

eyes of a customer. He would stroll through the facility and recommend physical changes to the appearance of the front entrance, lobby and hotel rooms. He would listen to verbal exchanges and recommend protocol changes in how customers were greeted and moved through the check in experience. He would call the front desk to request hotel services and follow up by making operational changes to improve upon how they were delivered. Izzy's discerning ears and eyes were constantly alert for ways to enhance the customer experience and he turned that commitment into a multi billion-dollar empire.

Izzy was well known for building the bridges necessary to deliver an outstanding customer experience but his true genius was in his ability to identify the gaps in the first place.

PART II

THE PRESENTATION PHASE

In this second part of the book you will learn how to deliver *client-centric* presentations that *separate* you from the competition and *inspire* action.

Introduction to PRESENTATION

The second phase of the Gap Analysis Client Engagement Model© is the PRESENTATION Phase.

- Have you ever delivered what you thought was a perfect presentation and yet failed to get the business? Or,
- Have you ever lost business to a competitor who offered a lower price or a reduced commission fee? Or,
- Have you ever had a client respond to your presentation with *"leave it with me and I'll get back to you"* and he didn't?

If you answered *"yes"* to either of these questions then you've suffered the consequence of a failed presentation.

If the ASSESSMENT phase defines the product or service gap, then the PRESENTATION phase represents the bridge that spans that gap. Remember, everything you do and say during a sales presentation either accelerates or decelerates your forward momentum.

PRESENTATION TIP:

Remember, everything you do and say during a sales presentation either accelerates or decelerates your forward momentum.

The purpose of this part of the book is to show you how to accelerate a successful client experience by giving you the **insights**, **skills**, *and* **resources** *to deliver client-centric presentations that separate you from the competition and inspire action.*

A mentor of mine Jim Rohn once told me, *"To be successful in life, simply do three things well: Have something good to say, say it well and say it often."* A successful presentation delivers on all three fronts: *"having something good to say"* refers to content, and *"saying it well"* refers to structure and delivery. When you are competent in these two areas you get invited to *"say it often."*

Structure

Let's start off by addressing the importance of *structure*. Structure is the first element of an effective presentation. It refers to the framework that sequences the flow of your information. Everything you do and say must be sequenced in a way that incrementally moves the client forward toward the desired outcome he or she wants to experience.

In Chapter Four, you'll learn the most powerful way to structure your sales presentations using a whole-brain reasoning technique that appeals to both the logical and creative sides of the brain.

Content

The second element of an effective presentation is *content*. Have you ever noticed that you can say one thing to one client and he or she will feel utterly compelled to take action, while the same information delivered to another client will leave him or her completely uninspired? *Words, phrases, images*, and *evidence* that evokes a buying decision from one may equally discourage it from another. It all comes down to their respective fears and desires.

Fears and desires are the two key motivators in every client engagement experience. Clients move toward what they desire and away from what they fear. As we discussed in the ASSESSMENT phase, knowing your client's engagement style will provide you with insights into both of these key motivators.

In Chapter Three you'll learn how to align your presentation to the unique decision-making needs of your client.

Delivery

The final element of an effective presentation is *delivery*. After all, you can have the finest content available, formatted within the ideal structure, and yet lose clients because you were unable to *capture their attention, hold their interest*, or *inspire them to act on your message*.

We've all had the experience of enduring a presentation that elicited feelings of boredom, anxiety or frustration. The reason this occurred was because the speaker's content and/or delivery style did not align with our decision-making needs. The same holds true for the clients you engage. A presentation that is paced slower than your client's preferred pace needs will result in feelings of *frustration*. A presentation that is paced quicker will elicit feelings of *anxiety*. Neither of these emotional states will support a favorable buying decision, even if your product or service offering represents the ideal solution.

In fact, my experience confirms that the biggest mistake unskilled professionals make is that they design and deliver presentations to inspire themselves, NOT THE CLIENT!

> **PRESENTATION TIP:**
>
> The biggest mistake professionals make is that they design and deliver presentations to inspire themselves, NOT THE CLIENT!

Think about it! They say what **they** think is important, they provide evidence in a sequence that convinces **their** logical mind, they speak at a pace, tone, and volume that **they** themselves find pleasing. They are in essence presenting to **themselves**, not the client, and unless the client has similar content and processing needs, the presentation will fail to inspire a favorable buying decision.

In summary, Success Partners accelerate successful experiences during the PRESENTATION phase of client engagement when they:

- Demonstrate a viable solution to the client problem.
- Align their content and delivery style with the client's unique decision-making needs.
- Address their client's key motivators and overcome their fear of taking action.

The Acceleration Strategies that follow will provide you with the tools to master the second core skill of client engagement -- PRESENTATION.

The Presentation Phase

~Chapter Four~
Crafting Your Message

Accelerate your professional success with a message sequencing strategy that convinces logically and inspires emotionally.

⁓

"Tell them what you are going to tell them, tell them, and then tell them what you told them."
– Teaching Credo

> *"Before I refuse to take your questions,
> I have an opening statement."*
> – Ronald Reagan

LADIES AND GENTLEMEN OF THE JURY

In a court of law defense attorneys rely on a logical information sequencing strategy to convince their jury to return with a *"not guilty"* verdict. This sequencing strategy is structured using a logical and linear three-part format:

Part 1: The Opening
All sales presentations should begin with an eight- to eighteen-word statement that announces the purpose of your presentation. Known as the Statement of Intent (SOI), this opening statement might sound like:

> *"We believe we can get this property fully leased in the time frame specified. Let me show you how."* Or,
> *"Here's how our company can save you over three hundred thousand a year in operating expenses."* Or,
> *"I've put together an investment plan to achieve your financial goals; let me walk you through my thoughts."*

Now you'll notice, in each case, that the SOI announces the client's desired reality outcome. Just as in a court of law a defense attorney begins with an opening statement that points toward her client's acquittal, so too should you begin your presentation by directing your clients toward their desired reality outcome.

The SOI serves three purposes:

1. *To introduce intent:* This allows the listener to focus on what you are saying rather than trying to figure out what you are going to cover.
2. *To confirm direction:* This provides a clear destination point that your clients will recognize when you take them there.
3. *To establish a measurement criterion:* This provides a reference point from which to evaluate the effectiveness of your presentation.

You may have noticed that each chapter of this book begins with an eight- to eighteen-word SOI. This one was to show you how to *"Accelerate your professional success with a message sequencing strategy that convinces logically and inspires emotionally"* — fifteen words that identify purpose, confirm direction and establish a reference point.

Everything that follows the SOI should be the information or strategy necessary to take the client to that specific outcome. If it doesn't, then it simply doesn't belong in your presentation.

Part 2: The Main Body

When designing your written or verbal presentation, consider segmenting the main body of your presentation into three parts. Why three-parts and not two or four-parts? Because **three** reasons, **three** action steps, or **three** benefits is enough to satisfy your client's logical decision-making needs. A two-part plan is too shaky to support a big decision and a four (or more)-part plan can be too overwhelming and confusing to consider.

'Three' is the magic number. Just as an expansive bridge

requires three pillars to support its center span, so too does it take three pillars to support the client's logical decision-making needs.

PRESENTATION TIP:
'Three' is the magic number. Just as an expansive bridge requires three pillars to support its center span, so too does it take three pillars to support the client's logical decision-making needs.

Think about it: a homeowner typically gets three estimates before adding a new deck or installing a swimming pool. A car shopper typically tries out three different styles of automobiles before settling on one. The homebuyer, before writing an offer on one property, typically requires two others as comparables to help justify the offer price.

Retailers have long known about the 'magic of three'. Most products or services are made available to the consuming public in three choices. Gas comes in three different grades (regular, premium, and supreme). Automobiles come in three different models (base, mid, and high end). Airfares come disguised in three different classes (coach, business class, and first class). Even most sporting events have three different seat pricing tiers (floor level, mezzanine, and nosebleed). Why, because consumers want to have two secondary reference points from which to support one primary purchase decision.

This book follows this same principle. It is segmented into three main parts:

Part 1: The ASSESSMENT Phase
Part 2: The PRESENTATION Phase
Part 3: The NEGOTIATION Phase

Each of these parts is broken down into three sub-parts (chapters) and then each of these subparts is flushed out into sub-sub-parts known as 'Acceleration Strategies'. Why? Because the logical mind finds it easier to remember information sequenced in this delivery format!

Regardless of what product/ service presentation you deliver, you should sequence it using this formatting technique. A real estate sales agent might structure a listing presentation using the following three-part plan:

Part 1: Market Overview
Part 2: Strategic Approach
Part 3: Sales Team (and roles)

This particular three-part plan incorporates everything a homeowner requires to support a listing decision, plus it puts it into a logical sequence. Properly delivered, this sequence *"convinces logically and inspires emotionally."*

Part 3: The Conclusion

An effective conclusion consists of two elements: A *summary statement* and a *call to action*. The *summary statement* is simply a reaffirmation of your opening Statement of Intention followed by a quick recap of your three-part plan.

The same listing real estate agent might summarize his presentation by saying, *"John, I've provided an overview of what's driving today's market. I've put together a pricing strategy and marketing campaign that capitalizes on these conditions and finally I've introduced you to my team who will handle every detail of this transaction for you."* That's your *summary statement*! The words that follow are known as the *call to action* and are vital if you are to move the process forward.

The *call to action* does not always have to involve the signing of an agreement. In some cases a *call to action* might be to set up a subsequent meeting or to research additional information. The main thing is that you continue to move the process forward, by a large leap or a small step, depending on your perception of the client's readiness.

If it's not appropriate to ask for the business, then ask the client to take a logical next step:

"Why don't we get together at the end of this week to give you some time to discuss this with your partner?" Or,

"I can have that additional information for you by tomorrow. Why don't we get together at 4:00 p.m. to iron out the details?" Or,

"What would you like the next steps to be?"

A product or service offering without a *call to action* is incomplete and will fall short of its objective to inspire action.

It's like a golf putt that comes up short of the hole. It never had a chance. Putt past the hole! Be willing to go the distance by asking for the business or by requesting the next logical step be taken. After all, if you don't ask you won't get.

It's also important to consider that your *call to action* be tailored to your client's engagement style. You'll learn exactly how to do this in Chapter Five.

Although you might find a solid presentation structure to be uncomfortable to apply at first, there are nine tangible benefits to delivering a well formatted and highly structured product or service presentation. They are:

1. **You don't miss anything:** Everything gets covered because everything is sequenced in a logical order and serves a specific purpose.

2. **It keeps you on track:** It's hard to get off track when you are following a straight line. If you do get pulled off track, it is easy to jump back on and continue where you left off.
3. **It places you firmly in control:** An effective structure allows you to instantly shorten or lengthen a presentation as required by the client.
4. **It is replicable:** A structure provides a template that can be used over and over again. The only thing you change in a structured presentation is the content and the style of your delivery based on the client's engagement style.
5. **It is adaptable to changing needs:** If, during your sales presentation, it becomes evident that you need to spend more time on one part of your presentation than others, you can adjust accordingly.
6. **It is easy to follow:** Strong structure is like using GPS. It's easy to reflect on where you have been, identify where you are, and confirm where you are heading.
7. **It generates momentum:** Each part of the three-part plan moves the client incrementally forward, across the bridge, toward his/ her desired end objective.
8. **It is more professional:** If two people deliver the identical content, the person utilizing a superior structure will always be seen as being more professional.
9. **And finally, because of benefits 1 through 8, IT WORKS:** It produces tangible results! I've had entire offices, after adapting this structural template, confirm that they went from a 40% presentation success rate to 80% virtually

overnight.

An effective structure affords you a considerable edge by separating yourself from the competition and making it easier for your clients to say, *"yes"* to your product or service offering.

PRESENTATION ACTION PLAN

INSIGHTS:

Know that the client engagement experience accelerates when the information presented is logically sequenced and structurally sound.

SKILLS:

Apply a structure to your presentations that consists of:

- An eight- to eighteen-word SOI to announce the purpose of your presentation.

- A three-part sequencing plan in the main body to house your presentation content.

- A *summary statement* and a *call to action* to conclude your presentation.

The Presentation Phase

~Chapter Five~
Aligning Your Content

Accelerate your professional success by aligning your presentation with your client's unique decision-making needs.

༄

"In the right key one can say anything, in the wrong key nothing.
The only delicate part is the establishment of the key."
– George Bernard Shaw

> *"Just give it to me straight!"*
> – Director Buying Motto

ENGAGING A 'DIRECTOR' CLIENT

Director clients are quick to partner with professionals who recognize their active pace preferences and outcome-oriented nature.

There are five behavioral *keys* you need to consider when presenting your product or service solution to Director clients:

- They are *task focused*.
- They are *behaviorally active*.
- They fear failure.
- They desire quick results.
- They are influenced by your ability to *get the job done*.

You may want to read these critical decision-making keys again; after all, when presenting to a Director client the success of your presentation is dependant upon your alignment with each.

Director clients respond to presentations differently than other engagement styles. Here are six ways to align your offering to the unique needs of your Director client:

1. Align your *Statement of Intention* (SOI)
Begin your presentation with an SOI that promises a successful outcome achieved in a timely fashion. Remember, every sales presentation represents a bridge that spans your

client's product or service gap. In the case of the Director client, he wants your bridge to support a quick and successful outcome. *"Let me show you how our company can save your company $300,000 in annual operating costs,"* or *"Here's how my team will get your building leased up in the time frame specified,"* or *"Here's how I can double your investment in the next 6 months!"* These opening statements all speak to the needs of the Director client.

2. Communicate in a style that is *direct and to the point*

Directors do not want you to mince words, skirt issues, or dress things up for them. They expect you to tell it like it is, even if the news isn't great. But they also expect you to take responsibility for your actions and to be ready to execute at a moment's notice.

If you don't know the answer to a question asked of you, say so and affirm your commitment to find out. When responding to questions, replace weak words and phrases with direct and affirmative language. For Example:

	Weak		**Affirmative**
Replace	*I'll try to...*	with	*I will...*
Replace	*I'll see what I can do.*	with	*I'll take care of it!*
Replace	*Maybe (or Perhaps!)*	with	*Yes (or Certainly!)*
Replace	*I'm not sure.*	with	*I'll find out!*
Replace	*That's not my problem!*	with	*I'll take care of it!*

3. Support their desire for *quick results*

Your presentation should demonstrate how you will achieve a quick and successful outcome. The phrase *"Time is money"* is the rallying cry of the Director style group. They don't like to be put on hold, stand in line, get stuck in traffic or worse yet be presented to by someone who is taking too long to get to the point. Express check-in and checkout counters at hotels, airports, and car rental agencies were all established in response to this psychometric pet peeve. American Express created the 'Front of the Line' campaign to support this inherent desire for the Director to jump the queue.

4. Alleviate their *fear of failure*

Quite simply stated, Directors don't like to fail. A failed outcome plays against their ego identity. Your presentation should therefore reinforce the fact that you, your team, and your company are all poised to help your client achieve a successful outcome. By the way, of the four engagement styles, Directors are most inclined to award you the business if you are the leader in your respective market. They like to associate with those who they perceive as 'best in class'.

5. Convince with *factual* evidence:

Director clients are predominantly logic based and are therefore influenced by factual evidence, especially when delivered in an executive summary format. Pie charts and bar graphs that provide a summarized overview strongly align with their decision-making needs. Let them know you've done the research to justify your recommendations, but don't mire them in your findings during your presentation.

6. Align your *call to action*:

Gain commitment with a *call to action* statement that shows a willingness to get started right away while allowing them to call the play. A service provider might align their call to action with: *"My team is poised and ready to get started on this project—we just need you to give us the green light."* A success partner might align with: *"I can have this ready for you to pick up tomorrow at 10 AM sharp. I just need your authorization."*

Make a mental note to never force a Directors hand or apply a high-pressure closing technique, as they are not fond of others attempting to dictate their actions.

PRESENTATION TIP:

Directors are silently evaluating you on your ability to get the job done so make sure that you demonstrate competence and capability.

Directors are silently evaluating you on your ability to get the job done so make sure that you demonstrate competence and capability.

PRESENTATION ACTION PLAN

INSIGHTS:

Know that the client engagement experience accelerates when you communicate your product or service offering in a way that aligns with the unique *content, structure* and *delivery* needs of your Director client.

SKILLS:

Apply a presentation strategy that:

- Aligns with the Directors 'executive summary' *content* needs.

- Aligns with the Directors directional, yet condensed, *structure* needs.

- Aligns with the Directors fast paced and direct *delivery* needs.

> *"Engage me, acknowledge me and connect with me."*
> – Connector Buying Motto

ENGAGING A 'CONNECTOR' CLIENT

Connector clients are quick to partner with professionals who recognize their active pace preference and relationship-focused nature.

Here are five behavioral *keys* you must consider when presenting your product or service solution to Connector clients:

- They are *relationship focused*.
- They are *behaviorally active*.
- They fear *loss of influence*.
- They desire *recognition* and *acknowledgement*.
- They are largely influenced by *the personal connection they feel toward you*.

Connector clients respond to sales presentations differently than other engagement styles. Here are six ways to align your offering to the unique needs of a Connector client:

1. Align your *Statement of Intention* (SOI)

Begin your presentation with an SOI that promises an exclusive offering or an innovative solution. An example of this might be: *"John, you are going to love what I have to show you"*, or *"Emma, I've located the ideal home for you!"*

2. Communicate in a style that is *interactive* and *engaging*

Perhaps the biggest need for Connector clients is to feel engaged in the process. They like to be given the opportunity to speak their mind, so give it to them. It's also wise to budget plenty of time for your presentation, as they're not afraid to offer up an opinion to someone ready and willing to listen. Keep in mind that Connectors have a limited attention span and will therefore need to be engaged far more frequently than the other style groups. For the most part, Connectors love to laugh, so keep it light.

3. Support their desire for *acknowledgment* and *recognition*

Your presentation should sincerely acknowledge the Connectors accomplishments as they relate to your product or service offering. Connectors are ego based and appreciate being recognized for their accomplishments.

I once witnessed a commercial real estate agent begin her office leasing presentation to a Connector client with the following SOI: *"We think you have the sexiest building in town, let me show you how we intend to get it fully leased up with equally attractive tenants."* I thought it was a bit of a stretch for her to refer to the subject building as *"sexy,"* but the client didn't. He was sold the moment she uttered the word. She won the business handily over more experienced competitors, who had apparently failed to recognize and acknowledge the building's obvious physical attributes.

4. Alleviate their fear of *loss of influence*

The Connectors ego identity is tied to his/ her ability to influence others, and when you seek out your client's opinion, you align with that psychological need.

5. Convince with *stories* and *case studies*

Connectors are not known for their pragmatic approach or their attention to detail. Rather than facts or figures, they respond far better to stories and testimonials, especially if they're familiar with the project or person referenced.

6. Align your *call to action*
Gain commitment with a *call to action* statement that is both collaborative and enthusiastic. An example might be, *"We're excited about working with you and eager to get started! Are we good to get started?"* Note that this *call to action* sounds nothing like the one recommended to the Director client.

PRESENTATION TIP:

Connectors are silently evaluating you on your likeability factor.

Keep in mind that Connectors are silently evaluating you on your likeability factor. Sure it's important that you have a suitable product choice or service capability, but for them, you must be someone they'll enjoy doing business with. *"Do I like this person?"* is a question often posed by the Connector's inner dialogue.

PRESENTATION ACTION PLAN

INSIGHTS:

Know that the client engagement experience accelerates when you communicate your product or service offering in a way that aligns with the unique *content, structure* and *delivery* needs of your Connector client.

SKILLS:

Apply a presentation strategy that:

- Aligns with the Connectors stimulating *content* needs.

- Aligns with the Connectors flexible *structure* needs.

- Aligns with the Connectors interactive and engaging *delivery* needs.

> *"I don't care how much you know
> until I know how much you care."*
> – Supporter Buying Motto

ENGAGING A 'SUPPORTER' CLIENT

Supporter clients are quick to partner with professionals who recognize their deliberate pace preference and relationship-oriented nature.

There are five behavioral *keys* you need to consider when presenting your product or service offering to Supporter clients:

> They are *socially focused.*
> They are *behaviorally passive.*
> They fear *loss of stability* (change).
> They desire *safety* and *security.*
> They are influenced by *those whom they trust.*

Supporter clients respond to sales presentations differently than other engagement styles. Here are six ways to align your offering to the unique needs of the Supporter client:

1. Align your *Statement of Intention* (SOI)

Begin your presentation with an SOI that confirms an understanding of the client's needs and concerns. For instance: *"Mary, this proposal considers the objectives you've identified and addresses the concerns you raised earlier."* This conversational approach is an ideal way to set the tone of your presentation with Supporters.

2. Communicate in a style that is both *collaborative* and *respectful*

Remain calm and patient, at all times. Supporters do not respond favorably to a confrontational approach. In fact, aggressive posturing will cause them to retreat into a position of quiet defiance. They may not vocalize their resentment as loudly as the previous two profile groups, but don't be fooled—their resolve is just as strong. Assure them that you're there as a 'Success Partner'—not as a 'Sales Person'.

3. Support their desire for *safety and security*

Your presentation should highlight the safety features of your product or service offering and the associated benefits. Not only must the client feel safe with your offering she must also feel safe about being in relationship with you. Trust is a big piece of the Supporter puzzle so be trust 'worthy'.

4. Alleviate their fear of *loss of stability*

When engaging Supporters, take it slow. This group does not like to be rushed and are not comfortable with change. Supporters are risk intolerant and will shut down if they begin to feel overwhelmed. During your sales presentation, check in with them periodically. Ask if they have any questions or concerns after each main part of your presentation. If they do, answer them, and check in to make sure the answer satisfactorily addressed their concern before moving on.

5. Convince with *testimonial evidence*

Supporters are influenced more by the opinion of others than they are by facts and figures. A third party testimonial carries far more decision-making weight, especially if that person is personally known. Facts and figures are too impersonal to convince this relationship-driven client.

6. Align your *call to action*
   Gain commitment with a *call to action* statement that is both collaborative and low pressure. An example might be: *"Mary, if you are comfortable with my team and our commitment to this project, I'd like to recommend we take the next step."* A presentation that is too rushed or high pressure for a Supporter will inevitably lead to feelings of anxiety that will result in one of the following classic 'put off' responses:
   Why don't you leave it with me, or
   I just want to run this by my partner, or
   I'll call you when I'm ready to make a decision.

If you hear either of these responses, recognize it as the Supporters way of telling you that she is feeling anxious or frustrated. Unless you back off, you won't hear from her again.

PRESENTATION TIP:

**Supporters are silently evaluating you
on your level of trustworthiness,
so do what you say you're
going to do.**

Supporters are silently evaluating you on your level of trustworthiness, so do what you say you are going to do.

PRESENTATION ACTION PLAN

○━ INSIGHTS:

Know that the client engagement experience accelerates when you communicate your product or service offering in a way that aligns with the unique *content, structure* and *delivery* needs of your Supporter client.

○━ SKILLS:

Apply a presentation strategy that:

- Aligns with the Supporters reassuring *content* needs.

- Aligns with the Supporters moderate *structure* needs.

- Aligns with the Supporters steady and deliberate *delivery* needs.

> *"Just the facts ma'am (or sir)."*
> – Analyzer Buying Motto

ENGAGING AN 'ANALYZER' CLIENT

Analyzer clients are quick to partner with professionals who recognize their methodical approach and outcome-oriented nature.

There are five behavioral characteristics you need to consider when presenting your product/ service solution to Analyzer clients:

- They are *task focused*.
- They are *behaviorally passive*.
- They fear *making mistakes*.
- They desire *accuracy of information*.
- They are influenced by *their perception of your subject matter expertise*.

Analyzer clients respond to sales presentations differently than other engagement styles. Here are six ways to align your offering to the unique needs of an Analyzer client:

1. Align your *Statement of Intention* (SOI)

Begin your presentation with an accurate SOI that promises a specific tangible outcome. An example of this might be: *"Our Company can save you $328,000 in operating expenses per year. Let me show you how,"* or *"Based on current market conditions, your home is valued at 2.8 million. Here are the comparables that justify this value."*

2. Communicate in a style that is *logical* and *consistent*
Analyzers appreciate communication rooted in logic and reason, so be sure your presentation is sequenced accordingly. Also ensure that you check for agreement each step of the way; after all, if an Analyzer doesn't agree with one aspect of your presentation, they will certainly not feel comfortable giving you their business.

3. Support their *desire for accuracy*
Your presentation should be comprehensive and double-checked for accuracy. Make sure the information presented is current and obtained from reliable sources. A great deal of the Analyzers decision will hinge upon their perception of your professional standards and the credibility of your sources.

4. Alleviate their *fear of making a mistake*
The Analyzers greatest fear is of making a mistake. Alleviate this fear with a comprehensive overview of the product or service offering backed by a personal assurance or performance guarantee. Both approaches are effective at overcoming Analyzer buying anxiety.

5. Convince with *statistical* evidence
Once again, Analyzers are influenced by logic and reason. Provide them with statistical evidence to support your recommendations. *Facts*, *figures,* and *case studies* carry the most weight with this group because of their objective nature. *Testimonials* from credible sources can also be effective at swaying a favorable buying decision.

6. Align your *call to action*
Gain commitment with a *call to action* that appeals logically. With this group, decisions follow analysis;

therefore your *call to action* should be aligned with this systematic process. At the conclusion of your presentation consider asking, *"If you are in agreement with our recommendations, may I suggest we take the next logical step?"* By the way, the next logical step may mean establishing a follow up meeting, getting another party involved, or some other course of action. The main thing is that you end the presentation with a specific request to move the process forward.

PRESENTATION TIP:

Analyzers are silently evaluating you on your level of professional competence so ensure that everything you produce is of a high caliber.

Analyzers are silently evaluating you on your level of professional competence, so ensure that everything you produce is of a high caliber.

PRESENTATION ACTION PLAN

INSIGHTS:

Know that the client engagement experience accelerates when you communicate your product or service offering in a way that aligns with the unique *content, structure* and *delivery* needs of your Analyzer client.

SKILLS:

Apply a presentation strategy that:

- Aligns with the Analyzers comprehensive and accurate *content* needs.

- Aligns with the Analyzers highly linear *structure* needs.

- Aligns with the Analyzers logical and methodical *delivery* needs.

> *"If a client can't differentiate your offering they will defer their decision to price."*
> – Gerald Gordon Clerx

DIFFERENTIATE YOURSELF

One of the most profitable statements you can master is the one that responds to the client's request, *"Give me a good reason why we should give the business to you."* When a client is having trouble differentiating between product or service providers, this question will likely get thrown into the mix, and the quality of your answer will tip the decision-making scale in or out of your favor.

To be truly effective, a statement of differentiation must follow three rules.

Rule #1: It must be unique

If someone else is making the same claim then it is not unique. When FedEx came up with their company slogan 'When it absolutely, positively has to be there overnight' they were filling a gap in the delivery market. In this case FedEx used a point of difference that was based on a 'performance promise', however personal attributes, specializations and market expertise also make effective points of difference.

Rule #2: You must have proof

Steer clear of broad and generic claims starting with the words, 'largest', 'biggest' and 'best' as they are difficult to substantiate. You may not have to produce the evidence but you must be able to defend your claim.

Rule #3: It must address a key motivator

A key motivator is anything that causes a client to move.

Desires are 'moving toward motivators' and fears are 'moving away from' motivators. Your client's key motivators should have been elicited during the assessment phase of the client engagement experience. If your differentiator doesn't, in some way, eliminate a client's fear or support their desire then don't say it. Being the 'biggest' or the 'best' carries no weight unless it can be tied to supporting a client desire or eliminating a fear.

PRESENTATION ACTION PLAN

INSIGHTS:

Know that when clients can't differentiate your product or service offering they will defer their decision to price.

SKILLS:

Apply the differentiation formula in this chapter to create a meaningful and compelling point of difference.

THE PRESENTATION PHASE

~Chapter Six~
Strengthening Your Delivery

Accelerate your professional success with presentations that are memorable and impact-full.

༄

"Think twice before you speak, because your words and influence will plant the seed of either success or failure in the mind of another."
– Napoleon Hill

> *"What we hear, we forget. What we see, we remember. What we do, we understand."*
> – Unknown

You've Got Thirty Seconds… GO

The average attention span of today's consumer is thirty seconds, which means active engagement is an extremely important part of any presentation. After all, a presentation that does not involve the listener is a lecture, and we all know how enjoyable it is to be on the receiving end of one of those.

Now, your client will not actually tell you that you have about thirty seconds before his/her mind starts to wander, but the evidence is incontrovertible. Think about it—the average news story, the average television commercial, and the average movie scene lasts no longer than thirty seconds. We have been literally conditioned to remain attentive for thirty-second intervals. After that our minds tend to drift to topics that we deem of higher interest or a more pressing nature.

During a presentation of your product or service offering, there are three ways to actively engage your listener:

Mental Involvement

Perhaps the best and easiest way to involve your clients is to ask them questions at strategic points of your presentation. Ask *open-ended* questions to gather information and *closed-ended* questions to clarify understanding or to confirm agreement. For those who need a refresher, open-ended questions are those that require more than a one-word response. *"What specifically are you looking for?"* is an example of an open-ended question.

A closed-ended question seeks a "yes" or "no" response. For example: *"So price is the most important consideration for you, is that right?"* Both questioning techniques serve a strategic purpose and should be used accordingly.

A second mental involvement technique is to request feedback or confirm agreement from the listener. Sample agreement phrases include:
Are we on the same page?
Are you in agreement?
Does this seem reasonable to you?
Are we aligned in our thinking?
Is this acceptable to you?

Not only do these questions involve the listener, they also let you know if your client is still standing by your side on the bridge you've just build for them. By the way, a great time to confirm agreement is at the conclusion of each part of your three-part plan. Once agreement has been confirmed, you have a green light to proceed to the next part of your presentation.

A third mental involvement technique is to have your clients see them benefiting from your offering. Pictures are far more powerful than words and when the clients have favorable images in their minds, they will be more likely to turn that image into reality.

Physical Involvement

Now let's look at physical involvement. It was Albert Einstein who said, *"Nothing happens until something moves."* Granted, he was referencing the theory of quantum physics at the time, but likewise in your presentation it's a

good idea to keep your client moving, preferably toward the far side of the bridge. Give your client something tangible to hold on to during your presentation or, if feasible, give her something to experience personally. Examples of physical involvement strategies designed to get the client moving during the presentation phase of client engagement include:
   Food sampling (grocery store)
   Wine tasting (wineries)
   Test-driving (auto dealership)
   Personal fitting (clothing store)
   Personal makeover (cosmetic counter)
   Property showing (residential real estate)
   Property walk-through (commercial real estate)

Emotional Involvement

Finally, consider involving your prospective client emotionally. This can be a little riskier to accomplish because emotional reactions to identical stimuli will vary from person to person based on personal history. Words or images that inspire a sense of anticipation from one person might elicit anxiety from another. That being said, the safest emotion to elicit during a sales presentation is a feeling of *joy* inspired by relevant and acceptable humor. Humor connects people and stimulates the release of endorphins throughout the body. This naturally fueled feel good chemical is a great way to enhance rapport and reduce buying anxiety.

Make sure, however, that the humor is appropriate to the individual and relevant to the circumstances. Misaligned humor, however innocent, can backfire on you. The profile group most responsive to the use of humor is the Connector. Other favorable emotions to elicit from this profile group include feelings of *anticipation, excitement, status,* and *acceptance.* Supporters respond favorably to stories that evoke feelings of *compassion, collaboration,* and *contribution.*

The Director and Analyzer profiles are not fans of emotional involvement techniques. They're more interested on the rational side of the buying equation.

Summary

This concludes the PRESENTATION phase of the sales cycle. Assuming you have *tailored your content, applied a powerful structure,* and *delivered an impact-full message* then you'll naturally transition into the third and final phase of the Gap Analysis Client Engagement Model©, the NEGOTIATION phase.

In the next part of this book, you'll discover three sources of negotiating power and learn how to align them in your favor. You'll also discover the three stress sources of every deal, and how to respond to them when encountered.

PRESENTATION ACTION PLAN

O— INSIGHTS:

Know that the client engagement experience accelerates when you actively engage your client frequently throughout your offering presentation.

O— SKILLS:

Apply a variety of *mental, emotional and physical* engagement strategies when presenting your product, or service solution to your client.

O— RESOURCES:

Create your own resource! Prepare a list of appropriate *mental, emotional* and *physical* engagement strategies for your product or service offering and integrate them throughout your sales presentation.

Excellence in Action – PRESENTATION

> Watching the late Steve Jobs deliver one of his trademark product launch presentations was a lesson in the art of persuasion. Jobs had mastered all three elements of a successful sales presentation; relevant content (what is said); logical structure (how it's sequenced) and; inspiring delivery (how it's conveyed).
>
> Review any one of his product launch presentations and you will see how he skillfully applies the elements of the Gap Analysis Client Engagement Model© in all his product launch presentations. Let me break down his winning formula:
>
> ### Part 1 - Define the Gap
>
> When Jobs begins his product launch keynote presentations he always starts out by making sure everyone understands there's a glaring problem in the market (gap), requiring an innovative solution (bridge). What's interesting about this part of the presentation is that many audience members aren't even aware they have a problem … until of course, Jobs tells them. The problem is either a missing piece of the mobile device puzzle or an example of product obsolescence in the marketplace. Jobs gift was his ability to spot potential problems well before they became problems and create opportunities well before others could act on them.
>
> In the case of the iPhone product launch, the problem, as Jobs stated, was that the current phones on the market (Blackberry, Nokia etc.) had fixed control buttons that couldn't adapt to new applications. Jobs deftly pointed out that this was a *"major problem"* and by doing so created an instant gap in the mobile phone marketplace.

Part 2 - Introduce the Bridge

In this part of the presentation Jobs would introduce (with great visual fanfare) the solution to the problem he had just created. This segment always focused on the revolutionary new features and the corresponding benefit the user would experience. The features were always technological marvels and the benefits always pointed toward ease of use or to a new benchmark standard of product design or performance. In the case of the iPhone it was the *"bit map screen with multi-touch technology."*

Part 3 – Recommend Action Step

The final part of the presentation was to let you know just how to go about bridging your 'latest and greatest' Apple product gap.

… And "One More Thing"

Job's made a habit of concluding his product launch keynotes with the phrase *"Just one more thing"*. This statement is the presenter's equivalent of a 'free bonus gift'. It is a 'value add' statement that leaves audience members feeling like they got a little extra by attending.

On top of all this Steve Jobs had an unbridled passion for the products he developed. That passion was evidenced by his words, his vocal mannerisms and his gestures. On many occasions it seemed almost as through he was about to explode with delight at what he was about to share with his audience. Some of the passionate language he used during his product launch keynotes included:

"This is an incredible device!"
"The iPhone has just reinvented the phone."
"This is really hot!"
"It's unbelievable?"

"It is the thinnest 'smart phone' on the planet"
"It's packed to the gills"
"It's the best window on the planet!"

The Result

Steve Jobs not only informed his audiences, he engaged and entertained them as well. It was this combination, paired with Jobs obvious brilliance that made him such an effective presenter capable of inspiring millions to take action on his latest and greatest Apple product.

PART III
THE NEGOTIATION PHASE

In this third part of the book you will learn how to *strengthen* your negotiating power, *overcome* the three stress sources of every negotiation, and *respond* appropriately to tactics and cultural differences.

INTRODUCTION TO NEGOTIATION

The third phase of the Gap Analysis Client Engagement Model© is the NEGOTIATION Phase. If the ASSESSMENT Phase 'defines the gap' and the PRESENTATION Phase "bridges the gap", then the NEGOTIATION Phase 'closes the gap' by transitioning the client's into their desired outcome. Think back to the negotiations that you've been involved in during your sales career.

> Have you ever lost a deal because your client got cold feet or couldn't justify the buying decision?
> Have you ever lost a deal because, during the negotiation, your client became *anxious*, *resentful*, *frustrated*, or *hostile* and walked away from the negotiating table?
> Have you ever lost a deal because both negotiating parties became positional regarding price, dates, terms, or conditions of the agreement and you were unable to resolve the difference?

If you answered *"yes"* to any of these questions, then you've suffered the consequence of a failed negotiation.

The NEGOTIATION phase begins the moment a successful presentation has concluded. The moment a client decides to take action on your product/ service offering, the negotiation has begun and concludes only when the product has been delivered (or services rendered) and full payment has been received. This time frame can span a period of seconds, minutes, hours, days, or even months depending on the type of your offering.

The reason why this sometimes-expansive time period is still considered the NEGOTIATION phase is because the deal is still technically open to rescission. During this transaction period, something could prompt the client to walk away and collapse the deal. The good news is that there are only three conditions that will cause a deal to falter once it enters this phase. When you can competently respond to these three potential deal-breaking conditions, you take control of every negotiation.

Understand that in the NEGOTIATION phase, you are participating in either of two roles: *process facilitator* or *problem solver*. The role of the *process facilitator* is to simply facilitate the natural evolution of the deal, to draw up the agreement, to help remove subjects, to consult with planners, to arrange for delivery dates, to deliver signed agreements, to secure deposits, to handle fund transfers, and/ or whatever else is required of you. Your involvement is simply to direct the flow of a naturally evolving process.

Your fee is truly earned when you are engaged in the role of *problem solver* addressing the obstacles and hurdles (stressors) that decelerate the forward momentum of the client's engagement experience. While a modest amount of stress is considered healthy in a negotiation, too much of it can bring a deal to its knees. Your role is to ensure that both parties remain standing, walking, and talking.

This part of the book is devoted to providing you with the **insights**, **skills**, and **resources** *to overcome the three stress sources of every negotiation.*

In Chapter Seven I will identify the three negotiating obstacles that can stall the forward momentum of a client engagement experience. These decelerating conditions are known as *mental, emotional,* and *positional stress*.

Mental stress refers to client *fears;* emotional stress refers to feelings of *anxiety, frustration, resentment,* and *hostility*; and positional stress refers to differences in *expectations* and *needs*. The critical point to understand here is that if either of these conditions is left unresolved, you end up with a deadlocked negotiation.

In this section you'll learn how to recognize the type of stress present and identify its root cause. In summary, the biggest mistakes success partners make during the NEGOTIATION phase of client engagement are:

- They fail recognize and alleviate *mental* stress.
- They fail to recognize and neutralize *emotional* stress.
- They fail to recognize and resolve *positional* stress.

The Acceleration Strategies that follow will bridge these competency gaps by providing you with the tools to master the core skill of NEGOTIATION.

The Negotiation Phase

~Chapter Seven~
Recognizing Negotiating Stress

Accelerate your professional success by recognizing the three potential stress points of every negotiation.

༄

"You can't shake hands with a clenched fist."
– Indira Gandhi

> *"Speak when you are angry – and you'll make the best speech you'll ever regret."*
> – Henry Ward Beecher

THREE TITANIC DEAL BREAKERS

The three TITANIC deal breakers in any negotiation are *mental stress, emotional stress,* and *positional stress.* When either of these conditions exists in a negotiation, your role, as the success partner, is to recognize it, manage it, and then resolve it.

When you can competently respond to these three decelerating conditions, you take control of every negotiation you are involved in and will rarely, if ever, lose a deal. Let's drill down into each of these stress sources.

MENTAL STRESS

"It is a luxury to be understood." – Ralph Waldo Emerson

Mental stress is the first potential deal breaker. It is the decelerating condition that exists when a client's fears of taking action become stronger than her desire for the product/service itself. In an earlier Acceleration Strategy I asked you if you'd ever lost a deal to a client who suddenly got cold feet and couldn't justify the purchase decision. This is an instinctive buyer response when under the influence of mental stress, a condition that has compelled a number of qualified buyers to walk away from deals they should otherwise have transacted.

NEGOTIATION TIP:

In any negotiation there are three potential deal breakers: *mental* **stress,** *emotional* **stress, and** *positional* **stress.**

Fear is a powerful decelerator and can be triggered by a number of external conditions including changing economic times, market uncertainty, third party opinions, lack of trust, or a number of other catalysts. By the way, whose job is it to monitor and manage the client's level of mental stress? I hope you recognize it to be yours, because you'd be right— **IT'S WHY YOU GET PAID!**

EMOTIONAL STRESS

"Discussion is an exchange of knowledge; argument is an exchange of emotion."
– Robert Quillen

Emotional stress is the second potential deal breaker. This form of stress exists when a party to the negotiation gets emotionally worked up and refuses to move off his/ her position or disengages entirely. When I asked you at the beginning of the chapter if you'd ever lost a deal to a client who became *anxious, resentful, frustrated,* or *hostile* during the negotiation, I was referring to **emotional stress!**

When clients state, *"I already have an existing relationship with one of your competitors!"* they are experiencing emotional *anxiety*. When clients lament, *"you've got to be kidding me!"* they're experiencing *frustration.* When clients respond to your proposal with *"Your fees are way out of line,"* they are experiencing *resentment.* When a client says, "This is an absolute waste of my time," they have elevated into feelings of *hostility.*

Unfortunately, while under the influence of an emotionally charged state the judgment process gets clouded. It has been proven that the quality of decisions are directly linked to that person's level of emotional stress. When stress-free, sound business decisions are made; when stressed, irrational decisions are often made.

Whose role is it to manage the emotional climate of a negotiation? Yes, that's right! **IT'S YOURS! ... IT'S WHY YOU GET PAID!**

POSITIONAL STRESS

"Diplomacy is the art of letting someone else have your way."
– Daniele Vare

Positional stress is the third potential deal breaker. This condition exists when two parties to a negotiation cannot reach consensus on the *price, dates, terms,* or *conditions* of the agreement. A buyer who is not willing to come up to a seller's asking price or accept the vendor's delivery schedule is locked into positional stress.

Unfortunately, once battle lines are drawn, those standing behind those lines often become entrenched; and if the situation isn't properly managed, a deadlock will ensue.

So, whose job is it to recognize and resolve positional stress? Right again! **IT'S YOURS! ... IT'S WHY YOU GET PAID!**

JAWS OF DEFENSE

"One of my problems is that I internalize everything. I can't express anger. I grow a tumor instead."
– Woody Allen

When confronted by mental, emotional or positional stress in a professional setting, unskilled success partners typically react with one of four defensive response strategies. I refer to these instinctual responses as the '**JAWS of Defense**'.

JAWS is an acronym in which '**J**' stands for **J**ustify, '**A**' for **A**ccuse, '**W**' for **W**ithdraw, and '**S**' for **S**arcasm.

Justify refers to an attempt to legitimize why actions were taken or why they weren't taken. Examples of justification responses include:

"Well I did that because…"
"That is not what I meant."
"There was no way for me to anticipate what would happen."

Accuse refers to the assignment of wrongdoing to the other, or a third, person. Examples of accusatory responses include:

"Perhaps you should have been a littler clearer in your request."
"If your secretary had forwarded the signed documents earlier, we wouldn't be having this problem."
"Your purchasing agent should have thought of that before he agreed to the delivery schedule."

Withdrawal is defense by retreat, like the person who

walks away from a transaction out of fear, frustration, or sheer exhaustion. Examples of withdrawal responses include:

> "It's the best delivery date I can promise you. If it's not acceptable, you'll have to go elsewhere!"
> "If you aren't prepared to come up in price, you'll lose this deal,"
> "Look, why don't you call me when you are ready to make a serious offer!"

Sarcasm is the final response strategy. It is a blend of one part accusation and one part insult disguised as humor. Although typically reserved for industry colleagues rather than clients, its impact can be equally devastating. Examples of sarcastic responses include:

> "This sales advise coming from a person who hasn't done a deal in three months!"
> "I might find that offensive, if your opinion mattered to me!"
> "Look who suddenly became the expert, in **MY** market!"

Rest assured that none of these **JAWS** responses will do anything to resolve the existing stress. In fact, they have the opposite effect; they exacerbate the problem and further perpetuate the stress.

Think about *your* natural response habit when confronted by a stressed client. Do you find yourself launching into **J**ustification, **A**ccusation, **W**ithdrawal, or **S**arcasm? Or are you one of the gifted few who have mastered a singular response that offends equally on all four levels?

No need to feel bad about it—after all, to defend, as we learned, is human nature. The opportunity presenting itself, in that moment, is to recognize when you are locked in the **JAWS of Defense** and upon doing so, stop and replace it using a non-defensive response—the **ACRE Formula**©.

NEGOTIATION ACTION PLAN

⊙━ INSIGHTS:

Know that the client engagement experience accelerates when you recognize and respond accordingly to the presence of negotiating stress.

> *"There is nothing either good or bad, but thinking makes it so."*
> – William Shakespeare

RECOGNIZING *MENTAL* STRESS

Think back over the course of your sales career. How many times have you heard a client respond to your proposal with *"Leave it with me," "Let me think it over,"* or *"I'll call you when I'm ready to make a decision?"* What the client is really saying in each of these cases is that your presentation has left them with unresolved anxiety.

The Gap Analysis Client Engagement Model© defines 'mental stress' as the condition that exists when a client's fears of taking action becomes greater than his desire for your product or service ownership. When this occurs, the transaction will stall and not regain momentum until those fears are identified and subsequently removed.

Recognizing Mental Stress

Mental stress is easy to recognize when you know what to look for. Its presence is communicated *verbally* through words and phrases, *vocally* by changing volume and tone, and *visually* by hand gestures and facial expressions.

Verbal clues are the most obvious and are reflected in the types of questions a client asks. Here are some indicators that your client's forward momentum has decelerated due to mental stress.

Questions asked include:
- How much time are you going to spend on my project?

- How do you guarantee your work?
- What are some case studies that prove you can do this?
- What other projects have this team worked on in the past?
- What is your fee and how do you justify it?

Statements made include:
- I'm not familiar with your company.
- You sound like everyone else.
- Your fee seems high.
- It looks to us like you have too many other projects.
- We are too small for a big company like yours.

Mental stress can also be detected vocally. When your client experiences fear his vocal qualities shift; vocal *pitch* elevates, vocal *tone* turns more businesslike and vocal *pace* quickens. Remain alert to sudden changes in either of these vocal patterns.

Visually, mental stress is also easy to recognize. When in this state a client's brow may furrow, jaw may tighten, head may shake from side to side, fingers may tap nervously, spatial requirements may expand, and direct eye contact may lessen. It is noteworthy that, in most cases, these vocal and visual shifts occur at a totally subconscious level.

So, in all your future negotiations, remain alert to verbal, vocal, and visual clues that might indicate your client is experiencing mental stress. A second thing to consider is that underneath mental stress are the core concerns that support it. Core concerns are almost always expressed as fears; fear of overpaying, fear of making a mistake, fear of change, fear of the unknown, fear of failure etc.

The only way to overcome a client's underlying fear is by responding with the *evidence*, *action plan*, or *performance guarantee* that resolves it.

Evidence
Evidence takes one of three forms: *statistics* (facts and figures), *case studies,* and *testimonials*. Any of these forms of evidence, assuming they address the client's underlying fear, will effectively alleviate *mental stress*.

Action Plan
An action plan is anything you agree to do or suggest your clients do to alleviate their fear of taking action. Due diligence is an example of an action plan.

Performance Guarantee
The third way of overcoming mental stress is with a performance guarantee. A performance guarantee says, *"This is what I promise and here is what happens if I fail to deliver on my promises."*

Supplying the right evidence, promising to take a specific course of action or making a guarantee of performance, eliminates fear and allows the client to move forward with confidence.

In all your future negotiations, remain alert to the *verbal, vocal,* and *visual* clues that might indicate your client is mentally stressed. If detected, respond accordingly by using a four-step resolution strategy known as the **ACRE Formula©,** which you'll be introduced to in an upcoming Acceleration Strategy.

When you recognize and respond accordingly to a client locked in a state of mental stress you accelerate a successful client engagement experience.

NEGOTIATION ACTION PLAN

INSIGHTS:

Know that the client engagement experience accelerates when you recognize when clients become 'mentally stressed' and seek to uncover their underlying fears or concerns.

SKILLS:

Apply the following observation techniques to determine if your client is mentally stressed:

- Pay attention to verbal communication patterns such as *words used, questions asked,* and *statements made.*

- Pay attention to vocal communication patterns such as shifts in *pace, tone,* and *volume.*

- Pay attention to visual communication patterns such as *body posture, hand gestures,* and *facial expressions.*

RESOURCES:

Create your own resource by identifying all the statements you encounter in your business that indicate the client is mentally stressed.

> *"The real art of conversation is not only to say the right thing in the right place, but to leave unsaid the wrong thing at the tempting moment."*
> – Dorothy Neville

RECOGNIZING *EMOTIONAL* STRESS

The Gap Analysis Client Engagement Model© defines 'emotional stress' as the condition that exists when a client experiences *frustration, resentment, anxiety,* or *hostility* during a negotiation. When these emotions are present in a negotiation, the transaction will stall and not regain momentum until the root source of the emotion has been identified and addressed.

NEGOTIATION TIP:

When emotional stress is present in a negotiation, the transaction will stall and not regain momentum until the root source of the emotion has been identified and addressed.

Recognizing Emotional Stress

Just like mental stress, emotional stress is very easy to spot. Its presence can also be observed by your client's *verbal, vocal,* and *visual* communication patterns.

Verbally, the types of statements made and questions

asked evidence your client's level of emotional stress. Here are some examples that might indicate your client is in an emotionally stressed state:

Statements made include:
Your fees are way out of line!
We had a bad experience with one of your people and don't plan on using you again!
We have a strong relationship with one of your competitors.
I don't like using sales agents!
This offer is insulting!
I've been on hold for 20 minutes!

Questions asked include:
What are all these extra fees? Shouldn't they be included in the purchase price?
Why haven't you returned any of my phone calls?
How much longer is this going to take?
Why wasn't I told about this earlier?
What's the hold up?
Why on earth is this taking so long?

Vocally, an emotionally charged state is evidenced by an increased vocal *volume*, an accelerated vocal *pace*, and an abrupt vocal *tone*.

Visually, signs of an emotionally charged state include reddening of the face, intensified facial expression, spatial intrusion, more erect body posture, heightened breathing patterns, and more directional and assertive hand gesturing.

Once again, the core emotions underlying this form of stress are *frustration*, *resentment*, *anxiety*, and *hostility*. This condition, left unresolved, has the potential to kill the deal and compromise the relationship. Gandhi was right when he said, *"You can't shake hands with a clenched fist."*

The quality of one's decision is linked to his/her level of emotional stress. The phrases *"I'm out of here," "You're fired," "Take it or leave it,"* plus a few other choice words and phrases are all easily uttered while in the grip of a highly charged emotional state.

While mental stress is rooted in fear, emotional stress stems from a perceptual belief. The statement *"We had a bad experience with one of your people and don't plan on using you again"* is rooted in a belief about something that a person did or failed to do.

The statement, *"This offer is insulting!"* is *frustration* rooted in a belief regarding the perception of value. The statement "I don't like sales people!" could be *resentment* rooted in a belief that sales people are not worth the fee attached to their services. The question *"Why haven't you returned any of my phone calls?"* is rooted in a belief that you are avoiding or ignoring the client.

Just like mental stress, emotional stress must be addressed and resolved. Your instincts may compel you to defend your actions, when the proper course of action is to remain non-defensive and allow the client to fully express herself, regardless of how hard it is to swallow what's being dished out. This can be a difficult undertaking, especially if you feel the comment is unjustified. Emotional stress only begins to dissipate once the stressed client realizes she is being listened to non-defensively.

In all your negotiations, remain alert to the *verbal, vocal,* and *visual* clues that might indicate your client is emotionally stressed. If observed, respond accordingly by using non-defensive listening skills to uncover and resolve the root cause using the **ACRE Formula**© resolution strategy.

When you recognize and respond accordingly to a client locked in a state of emotional stress you accelerate a successful client engagement experience.

NEGOTIATION ACTION PLAN

○━ INSIGHTS:

Know that the client engagement experience accelerates when you recognize when clients become 'emotionally stressed' and seek to uncover their underlying beliefs.

○━ SKILLS:

Apply the following observation techniques to determine if your client is emotionally stressed:

- Pay attention to verbal communication patterns such as *words used, questions asked,* and *statements made.*

- Pay attention to vocal communication patterns such as vocal *pace, tone,* and *volume.*

- Pay attention to visual communication patterns such as *body posture, hand gestures,* and *facial expressions.*

○━ RESOURCES:

Create your own resource by identifying all the statements you encounter in your business that indicate the client is emotionally stressed.

> "The best general is the one who never fights."
> – Sun Tzu

Recognizing *Positional* Stress

The Gap Analysis Client Engagement Model© defines 'positional stress' as the condition that exists when both parties of a negotiation become positional regarding the *price, dates, terms,* or *conditions* of a contractual agreement. When this occurs, the negotiation will stall and not regain momentum until the underlying interests are uncovered and a collaborative solution is proposed.

NEGOTIATION TIP:

When a negotiation stalls due to positional stress, it will not regain momentum until the underlying interests are uncovered and a collaborative solution is proposed.

Verbally, positional stress is easy to recognize by listening to the types of questions asked or statements made by the client. Although positional stress is not always communicated in absolute terms, the phrases *"I must have," "I will not,"* and *"I refuse to"* are all clear indications that you are toe to toe with a client preparing for a positional battle.

Here are some examples of more subtle statements a positionally stressed client might offer up:

> *Your fees are too high!*
> *I don't agree with your pricing!*
> *I want a cancellation agreement!*
> *We've decided to do the work ourselves!*
> *We must have delivery by the end of the month otherwise we'll go elsewhere!*

Vocally, positional stress is expressed by an intensified volume and firm tone. Visually, it's most easily recognized by closed body language such as crossed arms, a rigid body posture and resolute facial expressions.

While mental stress is rooted in *fear* and emotional stress is rooted in perceptual *beliefs*, positional stress is rooted in a real need or a specific *interest*. The statement *"Your fees are too high"* might be supported by an *interest* in being treated fairly. The statement *"I want a cancellation agreement"* might be supported by an *interest* in keeping control of the engagement process. The statement *"We have decided to do the work ourselves."* might be supported by an *interest* in obtaining the best possible financial outcome. The question *"Are you prepared to cut your fees on this deal?"* might be supported by an *interest* in saving money or looking good to the senior partners.

The most effective way to root out the *interests* underlying a client's position is to reply to the positional statement by asking one of the following clarifying questions:

> *Why is that important to you?*
> *What are you basing your opinion on?*
> *What specific concern do you have?*

What do you hope to achieve by that?
Can you help me to understand your objective here?

Now clearly, it's difficult to remain non-defensive in the face of positional adversity. When confronted by a strong offensive position you will feel an urge to respond with an equally strong defensive position. Resist the urge! Fortifying your position will compel your client to do the same, and once your client gets stuck on position he will become less responsive to invitations of compromise or collaboration. In the face of adversity it takes far more strength and courage to respond non-defensively than it does to respond defensively.

When you recognize and respond accordingly to a client locked in a state of positional stress you accelerate a successful client engagement experience.

NEGOTIATION ACTION PLAN

INSIGHTS:

Know that the client engagement experience accelerates when you recognize when a client becomes 'positionally stressed' and seek to uncover the underlying interest.

SKILLS:

Apply the following observation techniques to determine if your client is positionally stressed:

- Pay attention to verbal communication patterns such as *words used*, *questions asked*, and *statements made*.

- Pay attention to vocal communication patterns such as *pace*, *tone*, and *volume*.

- Pay attention to visual communication patterns such as *body posture*, *hand gestures*, and *facial expressions*.

RESOURCES:

Create your own resource by identifying all the statements you encounter in your business that indicate the client is positionally stressed.

> "A diplomat is someone who thinks twice before saying nothing."
> – Anonymous

THE ACRE FORMULA©

Whenever you encounter *mental, emotional* or *positional* stress, you have a choice to respond either defensively or non-defensively.

NEGOTIATION Tip:

Whenever you encounter *mental, emotional* or *positional* stress, you have a choice to respond either defensively or non-defensively.

Obviously, the more productive response option, in a relationship-driven business is to respond non-defensively. The **ACRE Formula©** is a non-defensive response strategy that is *hard on the problem* and *soft on the person*. It can be applied to all situations of negotiating stress.

ACRE is an acronym in which the '**A**' stands for **Align**, '**C**' for **Clarify**, '**R**' for **Respond** and '**E**' for **Encourage**. The act of aligning with your client is the equivalent of verbal Aikido, the intent of which is not to oppose force but rather redirect the energy toward a deeper understanding of the problem.

The purpose of the alignment phrase is to position yourself next to the client rather than against them, after all it's very difficult to fight, or argue with, someone who is standing by your side.

An alignment phrase can be in the form of an *agreement*, *acknowledgement* or an *empathy* statement. For example:

> Agreement: *"That's a valid point!"*
> Acknowledgement: *"I can see you feel strongly about this!"*
> Empathy: *"I understand your frustration ... I'd feel the same way!"*

An effective alignment phrase diffuses lingering stress and encourages non-defensive dialogue.

The 'C' in the **ACRE Formula**© stands for **C**larify. The act of clarifying demonstrates that you are remaining non-defensive by 'seeking first to understand before being understood'. Effective clarifying questions will uncover the root source of the stress. For example, a client's statement *"That's my final offer!"* might be rooted in a difference in perceived value (mental stress), feelings of frustration (emotional stress), or financial constraints (positional stress), each of which will require a uniquely different response strategy to resolve.

In some instances the underlying root cause might be difficult to pinpoint. In this case you might have to ask more than a few clarifying questions before you get to the root of the matter. Once uncovered, however, you're face to face with the six-hundred-pound gorilla that stands between you and a successful client engagement experience.

The '**R**' in the **ACRE Formula**© stands for **R**espond. Your response must address the root source of the stress. If the client is experiencing mental stress then your response

MUST allay his/her fears with *evidence*, an *action plan*, or a *performance guarantee*. If the client is experiencing emotional stress then your response MUST address the unresolved feeling with an *explanation*, an *apology* or a *personal assurance*. If the client is experiencing positional stress then your response MUST be in the form of an *interest-based collaborative solution*. You will learn more about these response techniques in the next three Acceleration Strategies.

Finally, the '**E**' in the **ACRE Formula**© stands for Encourage. The purpose of the encouraging statement is to reestablish the forward momentum of your negotiation. Sample encouraging statements include:

> *"Does that seem reasonable to you?"*
> *"Does this adequately address your concern?"*
> *"Does that seem like a fair compromise?"*

In essence, the encouraging statement confirms whether the six-hundred-pound gorilla is still standing between you and the deal. If the stress source remains, then go back and re-**C**larify with a follow up question such as *"Well then what would it take for you to move forward with confidence?"*

The **ACRE Formula**© is extremely effective at overcoming all forms of negotiating stress because it **A**ligns the participants, **C**larifies the core issue, **R**esponds to the core issue, and **E**ncourages consensus.

So, the next time you find yourself facing opposition (from a client, resist your defensive instinct to **J**ustify, **A**ccuse, **W**ithdraw, or become **S**arcastic and instead remain non-defensive and **A**lign, **C**larify, **R**espond, and **E**ncourage.

When you make this conscious shift into non-defensive communication, you accelerate the client engagement experience.

NEGOTIATION ACTION PLAN

INSIGHTS:

Know that the client engagement experience accelerates when you respond non-defensively to a client experiencing any form of negotiating stress.

SKILLS:

Apply the **ACRE Formula** © when responding to negotiating stress:

- **A**lign with your client

- **C**larify your client's underlying *fear*, *belief* or *interest*.

- **R**espond using the correct approach to resolve the underlying stress source.

- **E**ncourage your client to move forward.

> *"If you're not listening, you're not learning."*
> – Lyndon Baines Johnson

ACRE ELIMINATES *MENTAL* STRESS

Once again, mental stress is the condition that exists when a client's fears of taking action become stronger than his desire for your product or service offering. Sources of mental stress can include economic uncertainty, lack of information, lack of product familiarity and lack of trust to name a few. Whatever its root cause, this condition will stall the forward momentum of the transaction and could ultimately derail the deal if left unresolved.

Let's take three mentally stressed statements and put the **ACRE Formula**© to work. Consider this first scenario: You are presenting your service offering to a client who looks at you with questioning eyes and states:

I'm not familiar with your company!

What do your instincts tell you to do? If you're like most, you'd feel compelled to defend the company you represent with something like, *"Oh we've been around for years!"* (**J**ustification). Now, **J**ustification of track record may well be required, but not until you **A**lign and **C**larify, because at this point you haven't yet established your client's underlying *core concern*.

Underlying this statement of mental stress is a number of possible core concerns:

1. Fear that you lack capability
2. Fear that you lack capacity
3. Fear that you lack experience

Using the **ACRE Formula**©, we would respond as follows:

Align:
Remember, alignment can be in the form of an *agreement*, *empathy* or *acknowledgement* statement. In this case it would be most appropriate to use an agreement phrase such as, "*It's true that our company is lower profile than our competitors.*"

That's all that is required in an alignment phrase. It effectively demonstrates that you accept what the client is saying and are not defending against it.

Clarify:
The next step would be to clarify your client's core concern with as many clarifying questions as required. The obvious clarifier would be "*Do you have some concerns about our ability to handle a project of this scope?*" If the answer is "*yes*" ask a second clarifier such as; "*In what way?*"

Let's assume the client is concerned about your *capabilities*.

Respond:
Once again, mental stress can only be resolved with *evidence*, an *action plan*, or a *performance guarantee*. *Evidence* would include facts, case studies and/ or testimonials. An *action plan* could include an outline of the work you will perform along with a corresponding time frame. A *performance guarantee*

would be a promise to achieve a specific outcome. In this particular scenario evidence would more be the most effective response option to address the client's core concern regarding your capabilities.

An evidence-based response might sound like: *"Fair enough! Let me show you some other projects our company has worked on that were similar in scope."* Note: three pieces of evidence are all that is required to alleviate mental stress.

Assuming your evidence was satisfactory, your client's core concern regarding your project capabilities, should now be effectively neutralized. To confirm whether this is the case, take the final step in the **ACRE Formula**© and **E**ncourage the client to move forward.

Encourage:
A statement such as *"Do these examples alleviate your concerns regarding our project capabilities?"*
If "Yes": suggest next step
If "No": go back to **C**larify

Let's try another one! In this case, a client responds to your real estate marketing proposal with:

It looks to us like you have too many other projects on the go?

Underlying this statement of mental stress is a number of possible core concerns. Examples include:

- *Fear* of falling through the cracks
- *Fear* of conflict of interest

- *Fear* of not getting the 'A Team'

Do your instincts compel you to defend your ability to handle your current workload with a response such as? *"We've got plenty of manpower to handle this project!"* (**J**ustify) or *"We've always carried a heavy workload!"* (**J**ustify) or *"You know what they say—if you want something done, give it to a busy person"* (**J**ustify).

Now while these responses may be rooted in truth, they might not address the client's underlying core concern, which can only be uncovered by asking a series of clarifying questions. Here is how the **ACRE Formula** © could be applied to identify and resolve the client's core concern:

Align:
In this case an acknowledgement response would be better suited than an agreement phrase or empathy statement. Therefore you might respond with: *"It's true we have a number of other projects on the go."*

Clarify:
Your clarifying questions should seek to uncover the source of the concern. *"May I ask what specific concerns you have regarding our involvement in these other projects?"*

Let's assume that the underlying core concern is linked to your ability to complete the project in the specified time frame. Now that this core concern has been uncovered, your response should alleviate this fear.

Respond:
An appropriate response might be: *"I can understand your concern. May I tell you how we are able to*

manage our existing obligations while assuring you an on time project completion? (Provide an action plan or a performance guarantee)."

Encourage:
The final step is to encourage the client to move forward with a statement such as. *"Does this alleviate your concern regarding our ability to meet your project completion deadline?"*
    If *"Yes"*: suggest next step
    If *"No"*: go back to Clarify

Alright, one more example:

Your fee seems high!

Underlying this statement of mental stress is a number of possible core concerns. Examples include:

- *Fear* of overpaying, for services
- *Fear* of looking bad to senior partners
- *Fear* of not getting good value

We've all heard this statement before, especially in these price-sensitive times. Do your instincts tell you to Justify? Resist the temptation and instead apply the **ACRE Formula**©.

Align:
What alignment phrase would you use? Would you acknowledge, agree with, or empathize with the client? In this situation an acknowledgement phrase would probably work best. *"I understand!"* is about the only way you can align with this statement.

Clarify:
In this case you need to understand the client's point of reference, so you might ask; *"May I ask who or what you are comparing us to?"* The client's response to this question will provide you with his point of reference. Let's assume the client's point of reference is a lower fee quoted by one of your competitors. This is a valuable piece of information to uncover; after all, if your client can't make a value distinction between you and your competitor then his decision will likely revert to price.

Respond:
Your response must prove a value difference between you and your lower priced competitor. An example might sound like, *"Let me show you why, although our fees are higher than our competitors, in the long run we represent a better overall value for you."* (provide evidence).

Encourage:
An effective encouraging statement would be, *"Can you see how our services will yield a better net result for you?"*
    If *"Yes"*: suggest next step
    If *"No"*: go back to **C**larify

The **ACRE Formula**© is remarkably efficient at alleviating mental stress but it takes time to master. Remember; **A**lign by *agreeing, acknowledging* or *empathizing*. **C**larify to uncover the underlying core concern. **R**espond with *evidence*, an *action plan*, or a *performance guarantee* to allay that core concern; and **E**ncourage the client to move forward.

NEGOTIATION ACTION PLAN

○— INSIGHTS:

Know that the client engagement experience accelerates when you use the **ACRE Formula©** in response to clients experiencing mental stress.

○— SKILLS:

Apply the **ACRE Formula©** when responding to mental stress:

- **A**lign with your client by *agreeing, acknowledging* or *empathizing*.

- **C**larify the underlying core concern of your client's mental stress.

- **R**espond with the *evidence, action plan,* or *performance guarantee* to alleviate the core concern.

- **E**ncourage your client to move forward.

○— RESOURCES:

Refer to a few sample of ACRE Formula © responses to mentally stressed statements. Go to **www.theGAPanalysis.com** and click on the 'Resources' page to learn more.

> *"Nothing lowers the level of conversation more than raising the voice."*
> – Stanley Horowitz

ACRE Diffuses *Emotional* Stress

Once again, emotional stress is the condition that exists when a client experiences the emotions of *frustration*, *anxiety*, *resentment*, or *hostility* during a negotiation. Each of these emotionally charged states could decelerate the forward momentum of the deal unless properly addressed.

Let's select three emotionally charged statements and put the **ACRE Formula**© to the test. Here's the first scenario: You've just contacted a client who has a requirement for your product or service offering. During your conversation the client states:

> **We had a bad experience with your company and don't plan on using you again.**

Underlying this emotionally stressed statement is a number of possible underlying beliefs. Some of them include:

- *Belief* that it was intentional
- *Belief* that it will happen again
- *Belief* that your company encourages bad practices

Let's apply the **ACRE Formula**©:

Align:
In this case an empathy response would be the most appropriate: *"I'm sorry you had a bad experience with one of our people."*

Clarify:
The clarifying question that needs to be asked is *"May I ask what happened?"* Now you might consider this to be a dangerous question because it could open up a Pandora's box of negative emotions. Guess what – the box is already open! At this point you need to hear the client out and do whatever you can to salvage the relationship. If you played a role in the 'bad experience' then you may have to own up and make amends. If you were not involved then you may have to offer up a concession or provide a personal assurance that it will not happen again.

Let's assume the bad experience was related to a late product delivery. Your willingness to hear the client out has gotten you a foothold in the door. The quality of your response will dictate whether that foothold turns into an open door to a second chance.

Respond:
In this case your response should be in the form of a personal assurance, which might sound like: *"We value you as a client and clearly this should not have happened. May I propose that we add a 'delivery guarantee' clause to our agreement to ensure that this does not happen again?"*

Encourage:
Finally, the encouraging statement might be: *"Would that demonstrate our desire to win your business*

back?"
  If *"Yes"*: suggest next step
  If *"No"*: go back to Clarify

Let's try another one. In this scenario a residential real estate agent has presented an offer to the seller. Upon review of the offer, the client responds with:

This offer is insulting!

First off, what underlying emotion is the seller likely experiencing—*frustration, anxiety, resentment,* or *hostility?* It could be either one but it is likely *frustration*. Let's put the **ACRE Formula**© to the test.

Align:
In this scenario would you align with an *empathy* statement, an *acknowledgement,* or an *agreement* phrase? I suggest it would be wise to empathize: *"I understand you're frustrated with this initial offer."*

Clarify:
Your first clarifying question might be: *"What aspects of the offer are you in disagreement with?"* If price is the primary issue, which it likely is, a suitable follow-up clarifier might be: *"What do you think a more realistic offer price should have been?"* A final clarifying question might be, *"What are you basing your opinion of value on?"*

The answer to this final clarifying question will provide you with the client's "value reference point." Keep in mind that in any negotiation, *perception is reality,* and the better you understand your client's perceptual reference point the more effectively you can respond to it.

Respond:
In this case your response might be to recommend a logical next step. *"Why don't we compile a list of recent transactions to verify true market value and prepare a counteroffer that is reflective of our findings? We have nothing to lose."*

Encourage:
Your encouraging statement might sound like *"Does that seem reasonable to you?"*
If *"Yes"*: suggest next step
If *"No"*: go back to Clarify

Are you getting the hang of this? Let's apply the **ACRE Formula**© to one final emotionally charged statement in which a client turns to you and emphatically states:

I don't like using sales agents!

Now your initial instinct might be to respond with something witty and sarcastic or to justify the value you bring to the table, but resist the temptation and respond using the **ACRE Formula**© instead:

Align:
On the surface this emotionally stressed statement might sound a little difficult to align with, especially since the statement minimizes your professional role. But let's set the ego aside and make an attempt at an appropriate alignment phrase. You might respond by acknowledging: *"Sounds to me like you've had a bad experience with a sales agent in the past."* Although this is an assumption, it will likely ferret out the root source of the emotional stress.

Clarify:
You might ask, *"Are you concerned that it might happen again?"* Hearing the client out may provide you with some insights into the actions you would need to take, or promises to make, to regain the client's confidence. Let's assume that the root cause of her emotional frustration is linked to a bad experience with one of your industry colleagues.

Respond:
In this case you might respond with *"I totally understand and while I can't erase the past, I can provide you with a written assurance that this won't happen again should you decide to partner with us."*

Encourage:
An encouraging statement might ask, *"Would you be prepared to move forward if we put this guarantee in place?"*
If *"Yes"*: suggest next step
If *"No"*: go back to **C**larify

When you apply the **ACRE Formula**© in response to emotional stress, you accelerate a successful client engagement experience.

NEGOTIATION ACTION PLAN

○━ INSIGHTS:

Know that the client engagement experience accelerates when you employ the **ACRE Formula©** in response to clients experiencing emotional stress.

○━ SKILLS:

Apply the **ACRE Formula©** when responding to emotional stress:

- **A**lign with your client by *agreeing, acknowledging or empathizing.*

- **C**larify the root cause of your client's emotional stress.

- **R**espond with *empathy,* an *apology,* or a *personal assurance.*

- **E**ncourage your client to move forward.

○━ RESOURCES:

Refer to a few sample of **ACRE Formula©** responses to emotionally stressed statements. Go to www.theGAPanalysis.com and click on the 'Resources' page to learn more.

> *"Our task is not to fix the blame for the past, but to fix the course for the future."*
> – John F. Kennedy

ACRE Resolves *Positional* Stress

Positional stress represents the one negotiating stress source that is not entirely under your influence to resolve because 50% of the position is outside of your control.

Remember, beneath all statements of positional stress lies the interests that support it. Let's explore three scenarios involving positional stress and apply the **ACRE Formula©** to resolve them. In the first scenario a client reflects upon your proposal and asks:

Are you prepared to cut your fees on this deal?

Before we apply the **ACRE Formula©** to this positional question, let's identify some of the possible underlying interests:

- An *interest* in saving money
- An *interest* in being treated fairly (matching a competitor's price quote)
- An *interest* in testing your negotiating skills

Now let's resolve it using the **ACRE Formula©**:

Align:
"I can appreciate you wanting to secure the best deal

possible."

Clarify:
"What did you have in mind?"

Now, you might consider this to be a dangerous question to ask because it seems to imply that you're willing to compromise your fees to win the business. But rest assured that a willingness to hear the client out does not imply agreement. In fact, you are simply gathering information from which to formulate a response. If your client's request is unacceptable, you can always counter it or decline it altogether. It's entirely up to you.

A subsequent clarifying question might include: *"What are you basing this request on?"* Let's assume the client's underlying interest is 'being treated fairly' because one of the competitors offered to cut their fees on the identical product or service offering. You now have a reference point from which to formulate your response.

Respond:
"Here is what I would be prepared to do... (introduce an interest-based proposal.)".

Encourage:
"Is this compromise acceptable to you?"
    If *"Yes"*: suggest next step
    If *"No"*: go back to Clarify

Let's try another one. Your client asks you:

Are you prepared to guarantee your results?

Align:
"I can appreciate you wanting my personal assurance."

Clarify:
"May I ask what kind of guarantee you're looking for and why it's important to you?" You might follow up with: *"If we could come to an agreement regarding this issue, are you prepared to move forward?"*

Let's assume the client's primary interest was in ensuring there are no unexpected cost overruns.

Respond:
Your response should be in the form of a collaborative solution that addresses your client's underlying interests. For example: *"I would be prepared to cap the price for this project if you would you be willing to ... (request a trade-off concession).*

Encourage: *"Would this be acceptable to you?"*
 If *"Yes"*: suggest next step
 If *"No"*: go back to **C**larify

Here is a final example. How would you use the **ACRE Formula**© to respond to a client who positionally states:

I want the vehicle delivered by the end of the week!

Align:
"I understand!"

Clarify:
"May I ask why you need it by the end of the week?"

Client interest: Immediate need for transportation

Respond:
"Given your current situation, I would be able to offer you a loaner vehicle until yours arrives from the factory. I'll have the shipment expedited, at our cost, so that you have your new vehicle by next Tuesday."

Encourage:
"Would that work for you?"
  If *"Yes"*: suggest next step
  If *"No"*: go back to **C**larify

Note that an interest-based proposal will not always lead to consensus, but it's up to you to give it a try. Unfortunately there will be times when you'll invest time to go through this collaborative process only to find out that there's no way to create a *"win-win"* agreement and you end up with *"no deal"*! That **can** happen and represents the one reason why a deal could fall apart once it enters the NEGOTIATION phase.

When you encounter positional stress, use the **ACRE Formula©** to **A**lign with the client, **C**larify underlying interests, **R**espond with an interest-based proposal, and **E**ncourage the client to move forward.

Initially the **ACRE Formula©** may seem difficult to apply. Like any new skill, it takes time to master. So take the time and commit the formula to memory. Sit around a boardroom table with your colleagues and throw out commonly encountered statements rooted in *mental, emotional,* and *positional* stress, then role-play your response using the **ACRE Formula©**.

It's a far better idea to master the **ACRE Formula©** in front of your colleagues than it is in front of your clients.

Responding to a hostile client by attempting to recollect what the '**A**' in the **ACRE Formula**© acronym stands for won't go very far in neutralizing the hostility.

NEGOTIATION ACTION PLAN

INSIGHTS:

Know that the client engagement experience accelerates when you employ the **ACRE Formula©** in response to clients experiencing positional stress.

SKILLS:

Apply the **ACRE Formula©** when responding to positional stress:

- Align with your client.

- Clarify the underlying *interests* supporting your client's *position*.

- Respond with a collaborative interest-based solution.

- Encourage your client to move forward.

RESOURCES:

Refer to a few sample of ACRE Formula © responses to statements of positional stress. Go to www.theGAPanalysis.com and click on the 'Resources' page to learn more.

Excellence in Action – NEGOTIATION

> In my mind, the best examples of organizations that have mastered the art of negotiating are Amazon.com, Apple and Costco. Why? Because they don't negotiate! Walk into any Apple retailer or Costco warehouse and try to haggle the price of your acquisition. It's not going to happen!
>
> These organizations have learned that by doing an excellent job at identifying the gaps in the market and then brilliantly executing on building the bridges, they don't need to. Negotiating stress rarely rears its ugly head:
>
> - *Mental stress* does not exist because of the size, strength and return policies of the organization alleviates any fears or concerns the client may have about acquiring the product in the first place.
> - *Emotional stress* does not exist because any problems or concerns are quickly and non-defensively addressed. It's hard to get frustrated with a company that operates under a 100% customer satisfaction service commitment.
> - *Positional stress* does not exist because the only option available is to do business with them or not. If you do choose to do business, it is on their terms … not yours. It's hard to become locked in a positional deadlock if the only option is to buy or not buy.
>
> In fact, this is the place that every retailer and service provider strives to attain. An environment in which sales/service professionals are so well trained at assessing client needs and delivering ideal product/ service solutions that their clients make buying decisions … without any reservation whatsoever.

The principles of the Gap Analysis Client Engagement Model© will take you to a similar place with your business.

The Result
The results, for each one of these organizations, speak for themselves in terms of both revenue generation and customer loyalty.

After the Deal is Done

Accelerate your on-going professional success by relentlessly fine-tuning your product/ service offering.

∽

*Every **past** client is a **current** reference and a **future** prospect!*
– Gerald Gordon Clerx

> *"Failure is the opportunity to begin again more intelligently."*
> – Henry Ford

How Did I Do

In this Acceleration Strategy you'll discover why it's so important to obtain feedback from the client's service experience and how to go about getting it. In his acclaimed book *The Ultimate Question*, author Fred Reichheld discusses the merits of asking one single follow-up question at the conclusion of each sales transaction: *"How likely are you to recommend my services to your friends and colleagues?"* The rating scale ranges from 0 (not at all likely) to 10 (very likely).

The response given to this ultimate question will reveal whether your past client is a *Net Promoter, Passive* (neutral), or *Net Detractor* of your product or service offering.

According to Reichheld, *Net Promoters* are those who respond with a 9 or a 10. They are responsible for 80% of all repeat and referral business. They are the quiet foot soldiers campaigning on your behalf actively endorsing you and your offering.

Passives represent those who respond to the "ultimate question" with a rating of 7 or 8. They don't actively endorse, nor do they actively denounce, your service offering. They are on the fence and won't hesitate to jump to whichever product or service provider offers them a better price or greater convenience.

Net Detractors are those who respond in the 0 to 6 range. This group is responsible for 80% of the negative things said about you, your service, and the company you represent. Not only do they cost you in a damaged reputation, they cost you in lost time spent hearing out and responding to their often loud and drawn out complaints.

The conclusion of any client engagement experience represents a huge opportunity to seek client feedback. Whether good or bad it's well worth hearing.

During my twenty-year training career, I've made it a habit to obtain workshop evaluations after each and every training program and I've been humbled on a number of occasions. Initially stung by any unflattering comments received, I soon realized that each of these comments was a gift in disguise. In the long run, this feedback has allowed me to continually hone my craft and improve every aspect of my course content and its delivery. As a result of this refinement process my live training workshops now generate a near-perfect 100% Net Promoter Score.

True greatness is achieved by doing, reviewing and taking corrective action on what's not working. The Apollo 11 crew discovered this fact on their journey to the moon. After the July 20, 1969, lunar landing, a reporter praised crew-members Neil Armstrong and Buzz Aldrin for their piloting skills in landing their lunar module in the exact landing site on the moon, 384,000 kilometers away from their launch site at the Kennedy Space Center. Armstrong responded that they were actually off course *"95 percent of the time"* and that the only way they got to their final destination was by constantly correcting for the fact that they were always off course.

Likewise your success is accelerated when you learn from your mistakes and take course-correcting action. A customer satisfaction survey provides this opportunity; so don't let your ego get in the way of asking for feedback. The only bad feedback is the feedback you fail to generate.

SERVICE EXCELLENCE Tip:

The only bad feedback is the bad feedback you fail to generate.

Just as the Apollo 11 crew was able to pilot their spacecraft to their desired reality destination, so too will you get to where you want to get to in your business by engaging in course corrective behavior.

One of my Australian-based real estate clients has instituted a policy in which the Managing Director of each regional office is required to personally conduct a follow-up satisfaction survey on their clients. This initiative has been extremely enlightening and has provided them with three significant opportunities to accelerate the growth of their business:

1. The opportunity to gauge the performance of their individual sales agents and teams,
2. The opportunity to obtain valuable third party feedback to help improve performance, and
3. The opportunity to convert Net Detractors (dissatisfied customers) into Net Promoters (satisfied customers) by taking the necessary actions to make good on failed service experiences.

So consider conducting your own satisfaction survey, or commission someone else to conduct it on your behalf. While you should not expect to generate a 100% response rate from those surveyed, those who do are sure to provide you with insights that you need to help you hone your craft and direct your customer service training initiatives.

I appreciated IBM's Thomas J. Watson's response when asked how to achieve success more rapidly. His response ... *"Double your failure rate."* Remember there are no such thing as failures; there are only current distinctions to support future successes.

SERVICE EXCELLENCE ACTION PLAN

INSIGHTS:

Know that the client engagement experience accelerates when you take the time to follow up and seek feedback from your client after the engagement experience has concluded.

SKILLS:

Apply a client satisfaction survey to obtain feedback into the customer experience and take action on the information you receive from the client.

RESOURCES:

Create your own resource! After each and every sales transaction ask your client for feedback then take action on what they tell you. Use these distinctions to course correct yourself into the top 1% of your industry.

SUMMARY

> *"Knowing is not enough, we must do.*
> *Willing is not enough we must apply."*
> – Johann Goethe

At the conclusion of every one of my live presentations I recite the above quote. After all, new skills and insights can only effect personal change if they are applied. Knowing them is simply not good enough.

Those who have applied the principles of the Gap Analysis Client Engagement Model© into their business have experienced dramatic results. Those new to the profession credit this training for launching their careers. Experienced professionals tell us this workshop represented a 'traction point' from which their careers immediately accelerated.

Personally, I love to hear these success stories and the immense joy and satisfaction that always accompany them. Some of these testimonials have been included in the following pages.

Now that you have completed this book, I consider myself a partner in your success. As such, I look forward to hearing about your own personal success stories as you incorporate these skill sets into your business.

Remember, we get what we want in life when we help others get what they want. My promise to you is that the content of this book will help you get both.

To your accelerated success!

Gerald Gordon Clerx

Speaking Engagements

Gerald Gordon Clerx has been called the 'client engagement guru' who truly practices what he preaches. He is consistently the highest rated speaker at any conference in which he participates. His *engaging, entertaining,* and *inspiring* presentation style make him one of most sought after speakers in his profession. The skills and insights he imparts are relevant and immediately applicable.

To have Gerald Gordon Clerx speak at your next conference, email keynote@thegapanalysis.com or call Shelley at 604.837.0289.

Praise from course participants

"When it comes to training in sales and negotiation, there is simply no one better than Gerald Clerx. Gerald has trained my brokers on several occasions both here in the USA and abroad and the results are profound and measurable. In addition to the skills transfer in his courses, they are high energy, interactive, and above all...fun. Gerald is wonderful to work with and makes himself available even when he is not "on the clock". It is with pleasure that I recommend Gerald to any organization looking to improve the skills of their people."

David P. - Managing Director - Los Angeles, USA

"Gerald's training series was an eye-opener and truly an inspirational experience for me. I have had the privilege to not only take part in 'BRIDGING the GAP' but also be able to witness the impact of Gerald's work over all employees of my company, sales and non-sales, who continue to benefit from this concept daily. The concept and the way Gerald

delivers it to graduates is one of the most influential tools I have ever experienced in my industry."
    Iglika Y. - Manager Retail Services - Sofia, Bulgaria

"I recently undertook 'BRIDGING the GAP' training series with Gerald Clerx over three days. It was the best single training session that I have ever attended and changed the way that I perform in my work environment for the better. Consequently, I am achieving results at work that I didn't think were possible. I would highly recommend undertaking the 'BRIDGING the GAP' training series if ever given the opportunity."
    Stephanie T. - Account Manager - Melbourne, Australia

"I have completed several courses with Gerald over the past 6 or 7 years and I can honestly admit I use the skills and techniques that he promotes in my business on a daily basis, as do many of my colleagues who have attended similar courses with Gerald. In preparing each pitch to win an appointment I continually find myself referring back to Gerald's advice; looking to both read my target and align my offering with what they are trying to achieve. I have found these strategies to be highly effective, winning us countless jobs that seemed unobtainable prior to our winning pitch.
    Anthony W. - Director of Sales - Brisbane, Australia

"Gerald is a fantastic presenter whose teachings have helped me excel not only in the workplace but also in my personal life. I look forward to taking Gerald's course for years to come."
    Ted M. - Sales Associate – Vancouver, Canada

"In 18 years in the industry I have participated in numerous training courses and workshops. The two courses of Gerald's

that I have participated in have been in have been amongst the most memorable. Very relevant content and great delivery. I look forward to the next one."
   Simon K. - Managing Director - Wollongong, Australia

"I had the privilege to hear Gerald speak on presentation skills and the use of personality profiling to maximize sales presentation results. I was overly impressed with his style of communication and his ability to engage me in to his topic. I wish we could have had more time with Gerald to learn even more. However, I was surprised by how much I took away from his presentation in only a short amount of time. Gerald has given me techniques to implement that have changed my business tenfold!"
   Melissa M. - Senior Associate - Reno, USA

"Gerald's 'BRIDGING the GAP' training sessions are the best I have encountered to date, as far as content and delivery are concerned. It was in fact the only sessions I have attended that accurately address the common issues professionals face accompanied by appropriate strategies to address them moving forward. The interactive components of this course were second to none. I currently use several of the techniques taught by Gerald on an ongoing basis and would have no hesitation in recommending Gerald and his 'BRIDGING the GAP' training exercises."
   Marcel E. - Sales Associate - Sydney, Australia

"Gerald's perspective on understanding the personalities of prospects that you may be presenting to, and his strategy for delivering a message, or "value proposition", has greatly improved my success rate in competitive pitches. Gerald's 'BRIDGING the GAP' structure has also helped me to guide discussions in meetings, and provide verbal answers to "on

the spot" questions in a way that resonates with my clients and prospects. I would recommend Gerald Clerx training over any other sales training that I have had in 12 years of working as a sales representative for multi-national corporations."
                      Alan D. - Sales Representative - Ottawa, Canada

"I attended a number of 'BRIDGING the GAP' training session which Gerald facilitated. Anyone who wants to improve their skill set in obtaining a better understanding on who their clients are, what they want and how to move them from their current reality to their desired reality, should make these training sessions a priority!!!"
                      Paul F. - Director of Sales - Sydney, Australia

"Gerald is an articulate, succinct, and inspired instructor who has broadened my knowledge and understanding of assessment, presentation, and negotiations. I have taken a number of courses from Gerald both on-line and in person. I consider all of them valuable learning experiences."
                      John L. - Sales Representative - Toronto, Canada

"I have undertaken numerous courses conducted by Gerald Clerx. The course relating to ENGAGEMENT STYLES profiling was very interesting and Gerald was able to provide real life examples of how this has worked for him. This course was informative and I was able to take away tools that I could use not only at work but also in my personal life. Gerald's style of coaching/ training is second to none. He is interactive with the class, humorous and likeable. I have no hesitation in recommending Gerald as a trainer and I will continue to undertake his courses throughout my career."
                      Amanda A. - Account Manager - Melbourne, Australia

"Gerald's 'BRIDGING the GAP' seminar is an excellent tool for Success partners. It opened my eyes to how I was running my business currently and what I needed to implement into my day-to-day business to get the results I am looking for. A very worthwhile experience!"
     Adam K. - Vice President, NIS - Toronto Canada

"This was my second course with Gerald and I have to say that he has a unique ability to transfer the knowledge and experience, enough to positively energize all of the people he comes in contact with. Although extremely technically minded Gerald has the ability to communicate with simple, friendly language with a great sense of humor."
     Kreso R. - Client Manager - Zagreb, Croatia

"I have had the privilege of being trained by Gerald on several different courses, these training sessions have all been entertaining, informative and most of all productive which has resulted in my career accelerating to new levels. In recent times I have found the formulas taught through the courses to be invaluable in setting me apart from my competitors and allowing me to continue to grow my business and brand in a tighter market. I have no hesitation in recommending any of Gerald's courses to anyone!"
     Paul T. - Director of Sales - Adelaide, Australia

"Gerald is a difference maker! His 'BRIDGING the GAP' workshop was incredibly helpful and will be the driver behind our office winning more pitches."
     Yumi P. - Sales Associate - Indiana, USA

"If you get the chance to participate in any of Gerald's courses I would highly recommend the opportunity. I recently participated in Gerald's 'BRIDGING the GAP' seminar for a second time and highly recommended anyone whose business is client driven to participate in this course. The course provides an excellent structure and flow which allows us to help our clients bridge their gaps when it comes to their needs. Gerald's presentation skills keep the group fully active and engaged in the entire days program which is hard to do with a large group, over a extended period of time."

                Matt S. - Senior Associate - Vancouver, Canada

"Gerald's 'BRIDGING the GAP' training was probably one of the most memorable that I have attended, not only because Gerald is very talented presenter who connects with the audience in an instant, moreover because the course has changed my ability to win deals and gain partners forever. I have attended Gerald's course 3 times and every time I learn something new and valuable for me as a person and professional."

                Verka P. - Manager Client Services - Sofia, Bulgaria

"Gerald, I recently went back to a client of mine in Bucharest, Romania. When I walked into his office I noticed that a presentation that I had submitted to him over a year ago was prominently displayed on his office bureau. When I asked why he still had my presentation out on display he replied "I use it as a constant reminder to myself of what an outstanding presentation should look like."

                Blake H. - Sales Associate - Bucharest, Romania

Made in the USA
San Bernardino, CA
09 July 2018